Breaking Ceilings

Your Company's Blueprint for Achieving
True Sustainable Growth

TARIQ A. AMRO

PASSIONPRENEUR
PUBLISHING

Publishing information
Publishing, design, and production facilitated by Passionpreneur Publishing
www.PassionpreneurPublishing.com

Content developed using the support of the Ultimate 48 Hour Author
www.48HourAuthor.me

Tel: 1 300 664 006
Diamond Creek
Melbourne, Victoria
Australia 3089

DEDICATION

To my loving family, my sunshine, without you it would not be...

Testimonials

Breaking Ceilings is an excellent read! It is an easy to follow, yet powerful guide for business owners who are trying to find their way. Tariq is able to get to the root causes of failure and provides a road map for success.

Mohamed Kaissi, President ACFE Lebanon Chapter

This book is one of the best that I have come across that provides a clear simple easy road map to follow for entrepreneurs to guide them in building a profitable and sustainable business. Many of us will recognize these concepts which come across as simple and yet are the keys to running any successful business and unfortunately elude so many people. The explanations and writing are guaranteed to help the reader develop and implement their own strategy to ensure success for their business. A must read for leaders aspiring to take their dreams to the next level.

Owen Purcell, Managing Partner, EY EMEIA Mercury

CONTENTS

ACKNOWLEDGEMENTS

Writing this book was a journey that would not have happened without the patience, support, and encouragement of many people; thank you, All! I am truly grateful to have you in my life.

My never-ending gratitude to my wife, Dana. Your love, patience, and endless support, without which life would not be the same.

To Moustafa Hamawi, for boundless energy and helping me realize a dream a lot sooner than I imagined.

To Natasa and Stuart Denman and the 48-hour Author team, for the guidance on how to launch and complete this project.

For the encouragement and support, my thanks to Mohamed Kaissi, Tamer Amr, Ruba Qalyoubi, and Owen Purcell.

Last but not least, a great thank-you to Nadine Al-Sarraj for her superb editing skills, patience, and perseverance.

INTRODUCTION

Growth for the sake of growth is the ideology of the cancer cell.

—Edward Abiey, Author and Environmental Advocate

Small and medium businesses (SMBs) today are facing an ever-increasing list of pressures hindering their growth, be it industry disruptors, shifting consumer demands, workforce expectations, or social media. The head of an SMB today will need to think and act with more resilience to keep up with the pace of both challenges and opportunities, especially those SMBs with low tolerance to bad decisions.

Yet, and despite all these challenges, owning and running a successful business is something most people dream of. Some dare to go after it and a few actually achieve it. Not for the faint of heart, business owner-ship requires a marked level of commitment, sacrifice, and effort. While successful business owners may differ on the exact mix of skills, talents, habits, and elements needed to create and sustain a thriving business, they all agree that being in a state of growth is crucial for survival. The old question rings true: Are you green and growing or ripe and rotting?

If you think about it, every progress achieved, from the dawn of civiliza-tion to date, is centered around growth. That alone forces a more difficult question: growth in what? Is it in top line (revenue) or bottom line (profit)? Assets? Cash? Number of users? Market share? One may argue that all these areas are summarily represented in revenue and profit, and that's what business growth should be. But history is filled with remarkable examples of companies that have achieved substantial growth in revenue and profit only to crumble shortly thereafter, due to mismanagement, dis-ruptors, or fraud.

In essence, that is what this book addresses: how can SMB owners/managers sustain their company and drive it to grow *out* of being a small or medium business. *Breaking Ceilings* seeks to challenge some common misconceptions of business today and introduce the concept of *"True Sustainable Growth."*

Growth should be looked at from 3 key dimensions:

> How *True* is it
> How *Sustainable* is it
> How *Personal* is it

Growth is *TRUE*

It does seem odd for truth to be a dimension in defining growth. Isn't all growth true growth? Actually, no, it is not. Growth could have come from fraudulent business practices or by hiking up the price of products essential for keeping people alive, the way that Valeant, a drug company, increased the prices of some life essential drugs by 3,000%. Sure, it is growth (and quite lucrative at that), but is it *true growth*?

Growth through the value it creates for its stakeholders is an example of true growth: its customers, shareholders, employees, community, etc. True growth is based on ethical principles and rooted in good practices. Would you consider the creative accounting practices at Enron as growth? The pyramid scheme of Bernard Madoff as growth? Media coverage worldwide showed these to be fraudulent and therefore not true growth.

Growth is *SUSTAINABLE*

Every business owner launches their business with the vision that it will outlive them, yet few prepare their business to do so. The longevity of a business, or what is referred to here as the *sustainability* of a business, is a coveted goal. In other words, to have a sustainable business, there needs to be a sustainable source of growth, and to achieve that growth, the business must arm itself with the necessary tools and processes.

Growth through acquisition, while a seemingly speedy path to growth, is not always sustainable. In fact, it mostly isn't; mergers and acquisitions often fail to produce the results that they promised. This is mainly because we are merging 2 living beings into one body, or so the logic would dictate. In mergers and acquisitions, we overlook that we are trying to put 2 complete bodies—minds and organs included—into one. Our conviction in our surgical skills has us believing this would result in taking the best of both bodies to create our perfect new being. In reality, that approach to mergers and acquisitions has not often succeeded. Transplants, on the other hand, are a different matter.

Growth is *Personal*

Whatever you define growth as, it will drive your business. As Ghandi said: "Actions express priority." By extension, the personal dimension of growth becomes quite critical for achieving it.

Growth holds different meanings for different stakeholders within the company: dividends for its shareholders, pay and job satisfaction for its employees, more raw materials for its suppliers, and more value for money for its customers. The decision of what represents growth to an entity drives its entire being. That is why it is critical for its survival that this dimension be crystal clear.

Frustrated Business Owners

The statistics on success rates of a business vary considerably. The more prudent ones are listed below:

- Approximately 50% make it beyond the 5-year mark.
- Of those that survive the first 5 years, 8 out of 10 don't make it to the 10-year mark.
- Of those who survive beyond the 10-year mark are not profitable.

The statistics are disturbing and highlight simple facts: running a successful business is no easy task and not one to be left to the whims or gut feelings of its leaders. Keith J. Cunningham may have said it best: "Business is an intellectual sport; anyone who plays this game with their emotions, gut, and glands, gets killed. There is simply not a way to get lucky sustainably. 'Gut' is an acronym for *Gave Up Thinking*."

The concept of *Breaking Ceilings* was borne out of interactions with countless frustrated business owners over the years. Their frustrations had multiple sources; from issues with employees or the economy to systems, regulations, etc. I always believed their frustrations were valid, as regardless of their origin, they were all viewed as a hindrance to growth.

This book is for the SMBs who want to break through the multitude of challenges they face. Those leaders who want to be amongst the small percentage that make it beyond 10 years of operations, with sustainable financials.

This book will guide you on a path that will help you and your business:

1. Chart your own course, whatever you want that to be.
2. Revamp your company to compete at the next level.
3. Break away from the crowd of buzzwords and go back to basics.

Before You Start

As a university freshman, I was having lunch with an old family friend when he asked me, "What are you majoring in?" Business, I replied. *Business?!* was followed by a boisterous laugh, leaving me completely perplexed as to what he meant. Then he turned all serious, leaned in, and said: "Son, when I was your age, I went to visit my uncle. He was a very successful businessman in the agriculture industry. He asked me the same question I asked you, and I gave him the same answer you just gave me. Then the old man pulled me aside and said, 'Son, business is weighed on the scale.' You see there? You don't need to go to school for that." He laughed again and changed the conversation.

It took me years to understand those words. Simply put: you can study all the latest fads of business literature and techniques, obtain all the degrees in your chosen field, business will always come down to selling what you offer for more than what it costs. It is about making money; everything else is just a way to deal with the complexities of today's world. Probably your first thought is "Well, yeah, Captain Obvious!" True, but if it is that obvious, why do so many businesses open and close within their first 2 years? What about the billions wasted on systems and assets that do not generate any returns? Millions spent on marketing campaigns to the wrong customer groups?

My intention when writing *Breaking Ceilings* was to bring us back to the basics of business, to help business leaders focus on the things that matter and not be swayed by the latest fads of business, because no social media campaign in the world will save a company with bad customer service. A rebranding will not save your company if it is offering an inferior product to the competition, and paying high salaries to top talent won't salvage your sales if you are in love with your product rather than your customer. This book is not aimed at disproving business theories or practices. Rather, we will look at things from a different vantage point, cut through the fluff, and make some money.

The chapters of the book are organized under four sections as a journey:

1. Assessment—to triangulate where your business currently lies.
2. Destination—to help you set where you want your business to be.
3. Journey—to aid you in figuring out the path to get there.
4. Navigation—tools to help keep you on track.

Throughout the book, you'll note that there are forms and guides referred to. All these can be found at www.breakingceilings.com/forms.

Plan rigorously, measure constantly, lead well, and luck will be on your side!

May you continue to break every ceiling that you face in achieving your goals and dreams.

Tariq A. Amro
November 2018

ASSESSMENT

TACKLING PAIN POINTS—
WHAT'S THE PROBLEM

*We cannot solve our problems with the same thinking we used
when we created them.*

—Albert Einstein

The journey of a thousand miles begins with one step! But before we can take that step, we need to know where we stand. Similarly, for a business, before it can begin to chart its course for growth and expansion, or set a different strategy and business model, it's critical to understand what challenges are being faced today, both internally and externally.

Conducting a self-assessment is the best starting point to figure out where you and your business stand as well as to determine the multiple challenges faced. This chapter aims at guiding you through this self-assessment by using a 9-point evaluation system. Each area provides a different perspective as to where your business stands today. Think of it as a 9-point GPS triangulation.

1. Business Life Cycle
2. Industry Life Cycle

3. Value Proposition
4. Customer Profile
5. Competition Profile
6. Operating Model
7. Performance Management
8. Current Challenges
9. Attention

You can find a form that will guide you through the process at the end of this chapter or download a larger format for free from www.breakingceilings.com/forms.

Recommended Approach
Completing the self-assessment now will aid you as we move along through the chapters of *Breaking Ceilings*. It will serve as your reference point.

To strengthen your self-assessment, you will first need to share it with 3–5 people you trust within your business and have them fill it out on their own and then discuss it with them individually and collectively. Second, discuss the self-assessment with your "mastermind group." Your mastermind group is a group of 3–5 trusted advisors with whom you have an existing direct relationship. Third, the self-assessment should be completed in under 3 hours from start to finish. This last point is to ensure you prioritize key points and avoid overcomplication of the exercise. If you need that long to think about them, they are not top-of-the-list issues.

1. Business Life Cycle
Where is your business in the life cycle?

Life cycles are part of the natural laws of the universe. The Universal Law of Life Cycles states that everything born, if nourished properly, will grow to its peak and then begin to wither and eventually die. Businesses are no different; they too go through life cycles of birth, growth, decline, and, eventually, death. A prime example is the New York Stock Exchange. Twenty years ago, the top 10 companies consisted of car manufacturers and oil-related companies. Today, technology companies dominate, while some of them are barely a blip now. Everyone and everything is subject to the law of life cycles. This is not a reflection on a company's life-span, but rather it means that we need to be aware and plan ahead in order to prolong our business.

For small and medium businesses (SMBs), the difficulty increases. Ask yourself: why should your business live in perpetuity? Will it be the one to break the law of life cycles? SMB owners need to constantly question the relevancy of their business and push to plan for the future. If they do, then their SMB is on its path to breaking ceilings.

Why is it important to know where we are in the life cycle? Simply, if you don't heed the law of life cycles, you risk wasting countless resources trying to fix the wrong issues. For example, one symptom of a business in decline is falling revenue and customers leaving the business. The SMB owner's knee-jerk reaction is to push the sales team harder, believing the customers are leaving solely because they're not doing a good job with their sales. In reality, tackling the decline in revenue by increasing pressure on the sales team is tackling a symptom and not the cause! There could be a multitude of reasons—economy, product quality, or disruptors, etc. Knowing where our business is in the life cycle will give the owner a better understanding of the revenue problem and allow for addressing the root cause rather than the symptom.

In general, a business will go through 5 stages in its life cycle:

For each of the five stages, 2 dimensions will be explored:

First, the characteristics of each stage, which consist of team, money, records (accounting and bookkeeping records), the objectives of the business, the leadership of the business, and the corporate values.

Second, what to worry about during that stage.

A. Early Years
Characteristics

> **Team:** Usually a small number, informal
> **Money:** Tight and struggling to make ends meet
> **Records:** Poor, governance and systems are weak in general
> **Business Objective:** Survive
> **Leadership:** The owner is everything. It is a company of one, you are the one who essentially decides the way, and everybody relies on you for direction.
> **Values:** Corporate values are a reflection of the owner's values and work ethics. No formality.

What to Worry About

- The leader tends to have a limited understanding or differentiation between earnings (profitability) and cash. They confuse one with the other, because at this point, they are just looking to make the sale and get money in the bank. That is fueled by the fact that the leader or the business does not have proper accounting records or a system in place.
- The culture is slowly forming, and it's important to appreciate and be aware of it, because whatever is allowed now will be very difficult to change in the future. It is easy to compromise on values when the business is struggling to survive.

B. Rapid Acceleration
Characteristics

Team: Larger teams, some formality in place, a state of fluidity in the business where the organization structure keeps shifting and changing

Money: Revenue is growing, but unpredictable.

Records: Basic reports, income statement and balance sheet, limited management reports

Business Objective: The objectives of the organization are to ride the wave of fast growth as fast and as hard as they can. They're innovative in their products and services; they try and tackle the market, and they want to get noticed.

Leadership: The leadership team is formed, so you know who the key people within the organization are, but the key decisions always fall back to the owner.

Values: The corporate values are potentially fluid; some rules may be bent to allow for rapid growth.

What to Worry About

- Profits are somewhat neglected to make way for revenue, and while this is good for gaining market share, you have to keep a close eye on earnings. Good records are necessary.
- You are taking more risks in the business due to speedy expansion and potentially lower margins.
- The accountability is fluid; it is not clear who is responsible for what; governance is generally weak and considered low priority, but it does create problems in the long run.
- There isn't a decision system. It is really the owner by himself, and that can sometimes leave space for hubris and reactionary decisions. It is good to always consult with your management team on key decisions as well as for direction.

- Cultural values are important but sometimes overstepped to make way for growth; morale is slightly impacted.
- There is a lot of excitement due to growth in the organization, long hours, and some pressure that brings fuel into the business, but it may slowly impact morale.

C. Stable Growth
Characteristics

Team: The team size and structures are formed; there's a clear hierarchy.

Money: Cash flow is steady, and the ability to forecast product requirements is present, such as a twelve-month forecast with certain level of certainty.

Records: Reporting systems are well established and stable. They provide you with a monthly report; you have main KPIs (key performance indicators) within the organization; you're able to monitor things notably better.

Business Objective: Ride the wave; keep doing what you are doing, and try to maximize earning.

Leadership: The owner steps back to allow management to carry out their daily tasks, but still maintains ultimate control.

Values: At this stage, the owner wants to start setting some firm or formal values in the business, e.g. introduction of a code of conduct, corporate retreats, or staff and family barbecues. Efforts are made to formalize and influence culture.

What to Worry About

- Despite things moving in the right direction, and it being a stable state, this is actually the danger zone because the minute comfort sets in, the business starts neglecting the early signs of danger and decline that are popping up. This is where extra caution is required, not comfort.

- Senior management politics is quite high at this point. Because of the sense of stability, people become more territorial and choose to engage in politics rather than run the business.
- The owner goes through a very interesting phase, because they will either double the business and go into deeper expansion or they start questioning what's next. These are not necessarily bad phases, but if you, as the owner, are not aware that this has happened and do not have a good support system in place—be it through advisors or mentors—your business may potentially begin to stray to some strange places, and so this is where you need to be most vigilant.

D. Early Decline
Characteristics

Team: Some key departures, fairly stable team, senior management have been there for a while.

Money: Stagnation sets in; growth is very limited; it's down to the lower single digits at best, if not declining slowly. Cash flow is under stress.

Records: The records are well maintained; they're providing the necessary information.

Business Objective: Weather the storm.

Leadership: Owner is now paying close attention to what's going on, and there's a sense of anxiousness.

Values: Corporate values are deteriorating, fueled by a culture of blame.

What to Worry About

- Stagnation is attributed to external factors, like a recession, etc.
- Innovation is at its slowest point; the business is not coming up with any new products or improvements on goods or services offered.

- Worst of all, the blame is spreading throughout the business. The owner points the fingers of blame at senior management, the market itself, the customers, and the economy.
- Nobody is taking responsibility for what is transpiring.

E. Imminent Death
Characteristics

Team: Employee exits exponentially increase; frustration and anxiety set within the business.

Money: Profits are declining rapidly or already in heavy loss territory. Customers are dropping out.

Records: Records are somewhat maintained but not measuring the critical activities and their impact on the business.

Business Objective: Survive, back to the objective of the early stage.

Leadership: The owner intervenes to rescue the business; they become the sole decision-maker.

Values: Corporate values are now vague.

What to Worry About

- The owner refuses to accept that the business is on the verge of collapse and applies more pressure on the business to perform, assuming this will raise revenue and bring customers back.
- Cost-cutting initiatives are rampant, which is likely necessary but ill-timed. This will only increase uncertainty and anxiety within the business.
- Disruptors and/or competitors are gaining ground while the business is losing ground. Customers are moving away.
- Entropy is rampant within the business, and finances are under severe pressure.
- Transformation at this point is extremely difficult. Specialized help is required, and it is expensive.

Which stage is *your* business in?

2. Industry Life Cycle
Key Question: At what stage of the life cycle is your industry?

Industries, like companies, go through life cycles as well, albeit with different characteristics yet similar stages: birth, rapid growth, stability, decline, and then death. Industry life cycles are different in that they have a significantly longer life span than companies.

Examples of industries in Rapid Growth stage are the Internet of things, robotics, artificial intelligence, etc. They still have not stabilized and still have a huge potential for growth.

Stable industries have been around for a very long time, like FMCG (Fast Moving Consumer Goods). They are fairly steady in how they operate, and substantial growth is limited. Meaning, a business in an industry like FMCG will not be able to rapidly grow when compared to a business in the field of technology.

The idea is that it's important to understand where your industry sits, because if you're in a high-growth industry, then the potential for you to grow in that industry is also high. But if you're in an industry that is potentially stable or declining, then you have more limited chances of growth.

Recognize where you are, as that's what we need to focus on.

3. Value Proposition
Key Question: What is the current value to customers that your business provides?

Imagine being at a networking event. When introducing yourself, most tend to state their name, job title and company name, then elaborate on their product or service offerings. Notice this shows that most people define their business by the product or service that they provide and not by what benefits or value they add to their customers. Our rather simple question emphasizes a serious flaw in the strategy of most businesses. They tend to focus on the product and how it fits the customer instead of focusing on what the customers' needs are and whether their product meets those needs.

The first question in determining your strategy is "What is your Value-to-Customer *(VtC)*?" Simply put, without a clear *VtC,* your business will most likely struggle to get to the next level. Let's look at a couple of examples to illustrate the impact of a misguided *VtC.*

Example 1: Yoga Studio
Inspired by his love for yoga, Ben started his company "Bend Backwards." He was so passionate about yoga that you could feel the energy emanate from him during classes. He had a good marketing strategy, kept a close eye on his expenses and finances, and delivered great quality. He defined his *VtC* as his service: *Quality Yoga Classes.* Business was growing; people started talking about it, and prospects were looking good. But that was it; no matter what Ben did he could not increase his business beyond the capacity of his studio space and his physical ability to give classes.

Pondering his dilemma with a trusted advisor, Ben arrived at this critical sequence of questions.

Q: What value are we adding to our customers today (Current *VtC*)?

A: Quality yoga classes, easy-going atmosphere, reasonable prices, and convenient location.

Q: What must we become for our customers (Future *VtC*)?

A: Based on the data we gathered from our records, talking to customers, and competition, we must provide our customers with a "Quality Yoga, Fitness and Health Experience."

Thinking of the business from the Future *VtC*, it forces us to look at the business from an entirely new perspective. For example, Ben would start considering some other options such as:

	Additional Product or Service	What the Customer thinks
1.	Selling yoga related products, e.g. mats and bolsters, etc.	Convenience! Now I don't have to go elsewhere to buy this.
2.	Offering healthy snacks once his customers complete their workouts, or right before, to keep them energized.	Great, now I can have something healthy to satisfy my hunger.
3.	Different pricing structures that incentivize coming more often and at low attendance times.	Good, I did not like paying the monthly fees; now I can find a better fit for my budget.
4.	Striking a deal with other instructors to teach at his studio.	Variety! It is the spice of life.
5.	Installing a cryotherapy machine and offering discounted rates, if customers use it right before or after a workout at the Studio.	After a long day at work, I can energize my body before my workout or cool it down afterwards.

As you can see, the opportunities for expanding business start popping up just by changing how the company views its *VtC*. What quickly becomes obvious is that making some of the above changes requires a different set of resources, and it would be insane to think that you can make those changes with the existing level of resources and skills. Something has got to give:

1. Selling more products—this requires Ben to source these products or strike a deal on consignment with a supplier.
2. Healthy treats entail sourcing from another supplier as well as compliance with requisite health regulations. There may also be space constraints if his studio is too small and could involve some construction work to shift things around, possibly more machines, like juicers and a fridge.
3. Hiring an accountant to analyze potential pricing strategies.

4. Sourcing other instructors and someone to manage all their schedules.
5. Capital investment in a cryotherapy device.

The point to illustrate here is redefining your *VtC* will have pervasive impact on how your company runs, its supply chain, HR practices, financing, organization structure, and so on. Don't be fooled to think that it is only a small change. Remember, it has nothing to do with the resources that you have—it is about being resourceful.

Example 2: Plastic Bag Manufacturer

"Wrap Me Up" is a local plastic bag manufacturer that supplies bags to a large number of customers in the vicinity. Their *VtC* was "*Good quality bags at competitive rates.*" Their growth was stagnant for a couple of years. Their market share was healthy; yet they couldn't seem to increase their profitability or revenue.

Going through the same question sequence as in the "Bend Backwards" example, they could redefine their *VtC* as "*Helping our customer find the right packing solutions*"; then Wrap Me Up could potentially provide their customers with:

1. Customize quality to fit customer needs. Not all customers demand the high-quality, biodegradable durable bags.
2. Work with customers to better understand the different bag size required. So Wrap Me Up spends time with customers analyzing the size of their packages and coming up with creative solutions, as opposed to investing in production of bag sizes in lower demand.
3. Work with customers to find innovative storage options for their bags. For example, reduce shipment quantities and increase frequency or space-conscious packaging solutions.

Who do you think would win more work: the product-driven *VtC* or the customer-need-driven *VtC*?

Of course, changes to the company will be required:

1. Potentially a mathematician to work formulas for storage space capacity options
2. Increase in logistical support for trucks and frequency
3. Increased investment in research and development
4. Retraining their sales force

Figuring Out Your *VtC*

Identifying your *VtC* is both an exciting and frightening experience at the same time: exciting in that it will push you to see your business in a different way and frightening in that it will challenge what you already know and force select changes on you and your business.

Ideally, gather a small group of 2–5 people. Let's call them the mastermind group. They must:

a. Have the business's best interests in mind.
b. Know enough about your business and the industry that you are in, but potentially also about other industries.
c. Have trust and harmony amongst them.
d. Are not afraid to push the boundaries.
e. They could be advisors, employees, or if you dare, customers.

CAUTION:

> **Before you continue, please be careful. Going through this process and answering the questions below must be based on reliable data and reports, rigorous analysis, and actual discussions with customers (not through a telemarketer). Answering them from the gut, and having a lot of "I think" preceding every statement, will give inaccurate results.**

Now that you have your mastermind, you need to follow this simple 3-step approach:

- Current *VtC*:
  - What benefits do we provide our customers with presently?
  - What do our products or services mean to customers? What need do they fill?
  - How do we currently impact our customers? In what ways do we matter? What problem are we solving for them?
  - How positive have our results been based on the current benefits that we provide?
  - Are we satisfied with these results?
  - Over the last 2 years, have we been growing by more than 15%?

- New *VtC*:
  - What do we need to be for our customers?
  - What should our products or services represent to our customers?
  - What need should they fill?
  - Is that beneficial to our business? To what degree?
  - Are we asking the right questions to our customers?

- Changes Required (will help you in charting the course and determining the challenges, explained in later chapters):
  - What are the changes that we need to make to our business today, to change how we deliver our New *VtC*?
  - Do we have the right skills in-house to make the necessary changes?

- Do we have resources, i.e. funding for any unplanned capital or operational expenses, to support the changes?
- If we don't have the required resources, how can we get them?

At the end of this exercise, you should have a concise *VtC* that must be:

1. Clear: Can be quickly explained to anyone in less than 10 seconds.
2. Moral: It must be legal and ethical.
3. Precise: It has to be specific.
4. Purpose: It aligns with why you want to be in business.

4. Customers
Key question: Who is your ideal customer?

This is a potentially deceiving question that may reveal a great deal about your business. If you do not have clear customer personas (discussed at length in the chapter "Uncovering Customer Personas"), then unfortunately, your business is already at a disadvantage.

For the purpose of this self-assessment, let us start with the question of "who are you currently targeting?". Answering *"everyone"* is not practical and very dangerous. "Everyone" means that you are wasting sales efforts, marketing budget, and setting up possibly ineffective customer support facilities. A business is wasting money when it doesn't correctly identify its target customer.

Try and think of some attributes by which to describe your customers; you can begin with some basic demographics if you don't already have that figured out: age, income bracket, location, and buying habits.

5. Competition
Key question: How is your competition different?

Knowing your competition is important, but knowing how they differ from you is crucial to survival.

Start by listing the firms that you compete with. What characteristics do their products or services have? Are they more expensive or inexpensive than what you offer? Is their product or service of better quality? Are they part of a larger brand or a larger company? Or are they single, individual entities? Are they bigger or smaller than you? Why are they different from you? How long have they been in business?

The goal is to get a few clear, simple statements on how the competition is distinctive to your business.

6. Business Model
Key question: What are the revenue and cost drivers in your business?

Example: Revenue drivers for an outpatient clinic include the number of people receiving services, the type of services delivered, and the amount charged for delivering services. Cost drivers for the clinic include staff/labor costs, administrative costs, and facility costs.

A driver is a resource or a process or a condition that's vital to your business. It causes the revenue to be recognized, and the delivery of that product or service will trigger certain costs.

What are the critical drivers of your business? Or more specifically, what are your SMB's revenue and cost drivers?

7. Challenges
Key Questions: What are the key challenges facing your business today?

Think of the top 3 challenges or risks your business is facing. These could be external or internal or both. The goal is to be very clear about what the pain points are. These result in substantial frustration! They could be economic conditions, culture, the departure of several key employees, etc. Focusing on the top 3 will help you narrow down the number of challenges or risks.

8. Metrics
Key Question: What are the key reports and metrics that you track for your business?

What do you measure within your business to indicate its success? This is very important. Are you measuring operating cash flow? Return on assets? Revenue? Number of hours of service? Because what gets measured *gets done.* So if your focus is on earnings and only earnings, then your business will behave in a way that encourages improving earnings. That's not a bad thing, but if you neglect cash flow, then you will quickly run into a problem. This topic will be covered in the chapter "Unlocking Cash Flow Secrets." For now, please indicate in the self-assessment form what metrics your business presently focuses on.

9. Attention
Key question: What are the top 3 issues/concerns that, if fixed, would cause my business to thrive?

Finally, what needs to be corrected? From your perspective, what are the critical matters that need to be addressed in the business *today*? Do you need more capital? Do you need to improve your revenues? Is it the marketing team? Is it the overall marketing campaign? Whatever you believe is critical, please note it in the form.

While you are identifying the challenges and pressing matters, ask yourself: are these symptoms or are they core issues? It is key to differentiate between the two. For example, if you note that revenue is one problem on which you want to focus in order to grow, be cognizant that revenue is a result of activities and actions within the business. Revenue increases or decreases because of the particular marketing campaigns you adopt, the different product quality you have, the after-sales support, or pricing—each have an impact on revenue. What you must recognize in this case is that revenue expectations are a symptom and not a core problem. What happens in the organization and how it reacts to its surroundings are the levers you can use to impact and change revenue.

As you fill out the form, remember that this is a snapshot of where the business is *today*. The chapters in *Breaking Ceilings* are designed to aid you in changing the course of your business and achieve *True Sustainable Growth* for you, as the business owner, and all your stakeholders. Keep this assessment handy while going through the book; you will need it for reference.

Finally, the main doubts that need to be addressed:

1. You may question the process, given that there does exist both companies and family businesses that have been around for 50+ years. How is it that they have defied the Law of Life Cycles? This is a fine point. For those businesses that have survived for 50–60 years, there's a multitude of factors contributing to their extended life-span. Primarily, due to their acceptance of this law and their constant evolution to stay ahead of the decline stage. They likely have gone through a change in the operating model or developed a unique approach of appreciation for their customer or what their business specializes in. Meaning, it is impossible to sustain for so long with only a single, unchanging focus.

2. "What we've been doing works for us? Why do we need to change it?". Yes, it has been working for you; the question is, how long will it continue to work? The math is evident. Businesses in the small medium enterprises have a very taxing time transitioning from start-up to reaching the 5-year mark, and from 5-year to 10-year mark, and from 10-year mark to move beyond. Between 60 and 80% of businesses fail within the first 5 years. From those that succeed and remain, 90% do not make it to 10 years. And even those who manage to survive 10 years are struggling financially.

3. It is possible to sustain and live longer, but you have to look at things from an alternative perspective. That is the real meaning behind this book's title and aim; it's to guide so that you too are *Breaking Ceilings*. To help develop your business in a manner that allows you to continue to break these ceilings by perpetually evolving; changing; and building a distinctly strong, nimble, and agile organization.

BUSINESS SELF-ASSESSMENT

Company Name	
Assessor's Information:	Date
Name	
Title	
Relationship w/ Company	

Assessment Point	Short-form Answer	Description and Thoughts
Business Life Cycle		
Industry Life Cycle		
Value Proposition		
Customer Profile		
Competition Profile		
Operating Model		

Assessment Point	Short-form Answer	Description and Thoughts
Performance Management (top 3)		
Current Challenges (top 3)		
Pressing Matters (top 3)		

DESTINATION

MAKING YOUR MARK—
GOALS & OBJECTIVES

Objectives can be compared to a compass bearing by which a ship navigates. A compass bearing is firm, but in actual navigation a ship may veer off its course for many miles. Without a compass bearing, a ship will neither find its port nor be able to estimate the time required to get there.

—Peter Drucker

In keeping with the analogy of a thousand-mile journey that starts with one step, and now that you know where your business stands, we can take the first step, right?

Unfortunately, not yet. The key question is in *which* direction should the first step be taken, and that is determined by the final "Destination."

Setting a Destination for your business, clearly and without doubt, is the single most powerful aspect in driving a business and its leader. Another inspiring quote by Peter Drucker resonates remarkably well here: *"The best way to predict your future is to create it."* The importance of this step cannot be understated!

A word of caution is necessary. Setting the Destination for your business is a critical step in achieving a state of True Sustainable Growth. It requires thoughtful consideration, vision, and above all, unwavering belief in it! There is no Destination too big, too high, or too far if you, the business leader, believe in it. That belief will permanently guide you.

Setting the Destination

A treasure map is worthless if it doesn't have an "X" marking the treasure location. It would send treasure seekers on a blind expedition. Similarly, a business needs an "X" to go after, and this X has four corners. So, in setting the X for your business, there are 4 key coordinates that need to be clearly defined:

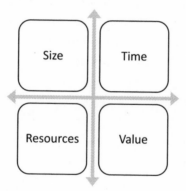

Size

When it comes to size, you need to be very clear about your target magnitude. The initial impulsive reaction is: I want my SMB to be large. Well, how large precisely? Are we talking $10 million, $100 million, $1 billion? Most would reason "I want a billion-dollar company." Fair. That is your right and can be achieved. But are you sure you appreciate your goal, and do you believe in it that much?

The best analogy I found to understand the degree of difference between a million-dollar company and a billion-dollar one is to translate it into seconds. Hence we have:

Time in Seconds	Equates to...
1 million	11 and ½ Days
10 million	4 months
100 million	3 years
1 billion	31 years

This comparison serves only to clarify and not to discourage, so as to allow an appreciation of the different efforts, resources, time, and type of thinking the two sizes have.

You can go for whatever figure you like; just keep in mind that your business must provide Value-to-Customer (*VtC*) in kind, for that amount. So the question that you should be asking now with your Business Self-Assessment (BSA) handy is "can my business deliver that much value at its current state?" If you're in an industry that is slow growth or if you're in a place where you're providing very little value to your customers, don't expect that you can realistically make the leap to becoming a billion-dollar company without increasing the value to your customers. Keep this in mind, regardless of the size you target.

Time

The second element is time. What is the time frame within which you expect to reach that Destination? If you're a million-dollar company today, and aim to become a billion-dollar company in 2 years, it is, while difficult, not impossible! You will need a considerable amount of resources and change within the business to achieve it.

It is difficult not to look at notorious disruptors like Airbnb or Uber, with their seemingly meteoric rise in their industries to become the giants in the market they are today. However, we should recall that Airbnb failed 5 times before growing to the colossus we currently know. It is too easy to neglect the total actual time that was spent for such entities to grow to their present-day size.

As we add the dimension of time to size, the X starts to take shape and a clearer picture of the necessary changes begins to form.

Resources

There are 3 key resources you need to consider when you're looking at setting a Destination:

1. People
2. Money
3. Culture. Yes, culture is a resource.

People

In order to reach your desired Destination of size within your desired period of time, a team is required. That team has to possess a certain level of skill, attitude, and commitment that is in line with the ambitious Destination. Consider, for example, you set the Destination to tripling or quadrupling in size within 2 years. How can that be expected to be achieved if you still have the same team, with the same skills, the same attitude, without any new training or enhancements to the organizational skill set? It is an impossible formula! You're putting the business in a very problematic position if you start pushing it to behave contrarily without changing the organizational skill set.

Money

Due to its scarcity, money is the first resource we consider, and usually about how difficult it is to get the necessary funds to expand the business. Our thoughts are most often around if the business had access to a certain amount of money, then it can do this or that.

Before we start thinking of the money we don't have, there are three pressing questions that need to be addressed (consider getting help from people specialized in this field; they can save you a lot of money, time, and pain):

1. *How much money does the business really need to get to the desired Destination?*
    Stress on the word *need*! Often a business owner may overexaggerate the funding required. This is mainly due to lack of thorough research and due diligence; we tend to overestimate what we don't know. As a business leader, you must dive deep into the details to figure out how much money is required. This cannot be a back-of-the-envelope calculation. If you do that, then yes, a lot of money will always be required. Get qualified advisors to support you with this, either from within the business, if you have the skill set, or from external parties.

2. *When is it needed?*
    Equally critical, can it be funded through the normal operations or are external funds required? If external funds are required, can it be done via a series of short-term loans that are quickly paid off, or is a longer-term solution required?

3. *What are you willing to give up for it?*
    This is the part that no one likes. Any type of funding, aside from a grant, means that you have to provide collateral, or equity, or otherwise. It behooves you to know what it is you are willing to sacrifice.

Remember, it's not really about resources; it's about *resourcefulness*.

Culture
Culture is everything. The way that you deal with your employees and your customers alike, your stakeholders, internal and external: think of it as the oil that runs between the parts of an engine. Is it a high-quality oil that

allows the engine to run smoothly, or is it a cheap kind that will eventually damage the engine?

Most people think of culture as a separate entity, but culture is necessary for the success of any strategy. If you have a perfect product with the perfect strategy, yet you have a culture within the organization that is rampant with bad politics, harboring no trust amongst the team members, and infighting, how can you actually realize that strategy and how can that product shine? It simply won't. Your organizational culture is such a powerful tool that, if harnessed properly, it can turn the tides in awesome ways!

My challenge to you is to consider culture as a resource, because if you design it and build it in the correct way, you will gain an immeasurable advantage. The closest analogy is underdog sports teams, who go from the last position to win the championship; what made that happen was the change in culture instilled in the team, plain and simple.

It's easy to say that you want a customer-centric culture, but do you have the processes to support that? It's easy to say you desire a culture of innovation, but are the systems in place to allow people to innovate and not be punished for failure?

Value
To become a billion-dollar company, you need to provide products or services worth a billion dollars. It doesn't work any other way. Value in this context means value delivered, and by extension of value perceived, meaning it is not about price and cost, but instead, providing your customers with what they perceive as value is what is worth a billion dollars.

Building on the Value-to-Customer (*V↓C*) discussed in the previous chapter, below are the questions to guide you through determining what your Destination *V↓C* should be:

- What do we need to be for our customers?
- What should our products or services represent to our customers?

- What need must they address?
- Is that beneficial to our business? And to what degree?
- Are we asking our customers the right questions?

Having a clear Destination gives clarity and focus throughout the entire organization. Even for junior level employees, it helps them know where the organization is going. They know the degree of size, the approximate time frame that they're under; they know the resource constraints that they face, the requirements, the type of culture available to them; this would influence their behavior to achieve that Destination.

Common Mistakes

Setting a Destination is no easy task; it is dangerous because a simple miscalculation may end up steering the ship into turbulent waters and cause it to sink. There are quite a few pitfalls that organizations stumble with. Here are the most common ones to be avoided entirely:

1. *Relying on the Mission and Vision Statements to be Your Destination*
   If you do a simple search online for mission and vision statements, choose a company at random and view their mission and vision statement. Likely, it's a vague, glossy statement that uses stimulating buzz words. At the end of it, you'll probably be left with no real understanding of what it is the company does, or how, and are less likely to see any indication of what they're trying to achieve. Though there exists a handful of exceptions to this, you will mostly encounter ambiguous mission and vision statements.

   Also, as part of your search you will find companies listing integrity, trust, quality, and transparency under their "values" description. This is a point I always find most concerning—shouldn't all companies already be striving for that? This is not really a goal to achieve, but rather is necessary for the SMBs existence. Such qualities or values are to be embedded within your organization. If you don't already have them, you should not be in business in the first place. That is why the mission-vision and value statements are generally overrated and a marketing gimmick at best.

2. *Too Ambitious, Too Quickly*
    It is the same as saying that you want your business to be a billion-dollar company in 2 years or less. Is it impossible? No. However, it is extremely difficult! It is a path filled with risks and requires massive resources and a fundamental change in thinking and attitude to achieve it. Be as ambitious as you want but appreciate what comes with your ambition.

3. *Being Too Timid*
    Fear is one of the most prolific killers of dreams and ambitions. Don't be afraid of wanting more. It is your right—go for it! But be realistic and understand the sacrifices and prerequisites associated with the volume to which you aspire.

4. *Wanting Too Much for Too Little*
    Simple put: To get, you must first give. To become a multi-million-dollar company, you need to give products or services to your customers that exceed that amount. That is how you ensure success. This is not to be confused with actual dollars. Meaning, you can sell a product for 10 times what it costs as long as the customer's perceived value of that product or service is equal to that amount. The customer needs to feel that they are getting a bargain.

5. *Forgetting About What Matters*
    Your Destination needs to include your employees and culture. Be very clear about 1) the type of culture and employees required to get to your Destination and 2) the type of culture and employees desired once you reach the Destination.

A business consists of employees, who are the backbone of any business, and the corresponding culture that runs through the veins of the organization. It is vital to include them; otherwise, you are gambling with the future of the business.

6. *Uniqueness*

   Imitation may be said to be the highest form of flattery, but this is not applicable in a sustainable business. Don't copycat. Set your own Destination. Let it be entirely your own and unique from anyone else's. It's imperative that you don't copycat, because the minute you do, you lose all authenticity.

7. *Being Too Vague*

   That's a death trap. Being too vague implies you have no Destination at all. You need to be very clear about where you want to reach; both employees and customers will not follow a business that does not know where it is going.

8. *Setting Too Many Destinations*

   It must be one Destination; you cannot be in multiple places at the same time. This will more likely result in a loss of the business's focus, as well as an unnecessary distribution of resources.

9. *Getting Too Comfortable*

   The Destination needs to be a stretched one—it cannot be a comfortable achievement. If you are content with a comfortable Destination, then that is a sign that you could be in the decline stage of the life cycle.

   You need to be stretching yourself and your organization beyond what is comfortable. However, keep in mind that you should refrain from stretching it to the point of breaking. Listen to your team, read your reports carefully, and keep an eye out for general signs of stress to determine if you are at the breaking point or not. Unfortunately, there is no clear instructions on how to figure out the breaking point. You just need to be extra vigilant in identifying early signs of stress.

10. *Non-Measurable Destination*

We mostly tend to outline size and time, because they are clear and easy to define. When it comes to employees and culture, though less straightforward to measure, they can be articulated. Feedback from your employees themselves or external assessments can be used to gauge the set characteristics or qualities you value in your employees and culture at the destination level.

If you can't measure where you are, then you can't use the navigation tools to assess your present standing and what degree of course adjustment is required.

Afterthought

All this talk about setting Destinations has probably left you with some concerns. Here are a few:

1. "Why can't companies just use the5-year plans they set for themselves and consider them as Destinations?" Well, that really depends., If the 5-year plan states where you want to go and is clear about the time frame, the resources required, and the value that you're delivering—then you're okay. But if the 5-year plan is just a projection of revenues and growth through a bunch of Excel sheets, then it's not really a Destination. It's wishful thinking!

2. "What's wrong with just milking it for what it's worth and then folding when the business starts to decline?" There's nothing wrong with that, but then you are subject to the circumstances, and you're not creating your own narrative for your business; you're not charting the course that you want to follow. It is important to set that Destination if you want to be in control and not just take what life offers you.

Next steps

Finally, a little bit of homework for you. At the end of this chapter is a form that will help guide you through setting the Destination. This is an exercise where you definitely need to include either your advisors or your senior management. I propose that you do both and craft your own Destination.

As an owner, you may face a challenge, because your senior team might not be so enthused about setting stretch goals; that is to be expected. Instigate an open dialogue and explain the life cycles to them and how, in reality, either you grow or you die. You will always encounter those opposed to change. Address them urgently—either they are on board or need to get off quickly. There is no room for negative attitudes. Your business will go farther with those who share the SMB owner's vision.

It is a collaborative effort, not something that you do on your own, sitting in your office and figuring out where you want to take this company. That's probably one of the worst things you can do, because rather than engaging your team and their excitement, you're just giving orders. You need to include them to bring up that momentum.

I leave you with this quote from David Schwartz: "Think little goals and expect little achievements. Think big goals and win big success."

Good luck!

SETTING MY DESTINATION

Company Name	
Assessor's Information:	Date
Name	
Title	
Relationship w/ Company	

VALUE (What value will my business add?)

SIZE (What size will my business grow to?)

TIME (When do I want it to happen by?)

RESOURCES (What resources do I need to achieve all this?)

People	Culture	Money

JOURNEY

UNCOVERING CUSTOMER PERSONAS—
CUSTOMERS & MARKETING

*The aim of marketing is to know and
understand the customer so well, the product or
service fits him and sells itself.*

—*Peter Drucker*

Answer this: if your life depended on knowing someone, how much time would you spend to get to know them? What would you do to make sure you understand their likes and dislikes, how they buy, their pains, their pleasures? The answer is probably that you would do anything and everything in your power to know them better than they know themselves, right? After all, your life depends on it. So, why is it that most companies don't realize that about their customers? Your livelihood, and that of your business, depends on intimately knowing your customers. Yet most SMBs are content with some basic demographic information about their customers and believe that it is sufficient to make their decisions. Simply put, you can never spend enough time knowing your customers.

To put that theory to test, we ask: *Do you know who your customers are?* If your answer is something like: "Our customer is *[insert gender]* between the ages *[insert age range]* residing in *[insert geography]* with monthly/annual income of *[insert range]*," you are in serious trouble. Segmenting your customers by only simple demographic data in this day and age is a recipe for failure and loss. Why? Well, because customer needs are changing rapidly; every other day another disruptor is emerging and pulling the rug from under the established businesses. Look what Uber did to the taxi business, Airbnb to hotels, etc. The only way to survive this rapidly changing world is to stay close to your customers or, more accurately put, *fall in love* with your customers.

When you fall in love with someone, you are enthralled to know everything about them—how they like their eggs, how they unwind, their favorite brands, etc. The benefits of being close to your customers are varied; in one way or another, they all manifest into cost savings, increased revenue, or increased market share. For example:

1. Customizing the product or service to fit the customers' actual needs or wants.
2. Targeted marketing campaigns instead of mass campaigns.
3. Concentrating R&D efforts based on customer feedback on what they like and dislike about your product.
4. Streamlining sales and product delivery channels.
5. Receiving early signs of changes in their habits and needs.

For those cost savings and revenue increases to actually materialize, a robust system needs to be put in place within the organization. Such a system would look something like this:

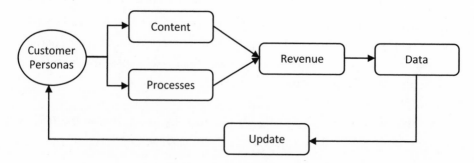

CUSTOMER PERSONAS

Customer personas are a way to segment the market, by gathering qualitative and quantitative data to build models of the target or ideal customers. Or, in more user-friendly terms, it is a predictive, data-driven model of customers that would help the business understand who its customers are and how they would behave. Donald A. Norman, of the Nielsen Norman Group, summed up the benefits of customer personas in his statement, "A major virtue of Personas is the establishment of empathy and understanding of the individuals who use the product." And that is the boon of marketing: to know your customers so well that the product practically sells itself.

Equally important is to understand the difference between market segments and customer personas. Market segments and customer personas have been used interchangeably, where although they may be in the same direction, they are different. Market segments are the broad concept, while customer persona is more specific to an ideal customer.

This comparison will better showcase the impact of customer personas:

Market Segment	Customer Persona

• Geography
• Behavioral
• Seasonal
• Benefits
• Demographics such as:
  • Gender
  • Age
  • Occupation
  • Income bracket
  • Family status
	• Jane is a senior accountant who graduated from a reputable university. She has been at her job for the past 5 years. Married with 2 kids, boy and girl, ages 5 and 8.
	• Her husband is a lawyer working in a firm downtown.
	• Combined income of $250K.
	• They live in suburb X and have a mortgage.
	• Financial planning is important to them as they would like to send their kids to Ivy league universities.
	• They mostly shop online because it saves them time and money.
	• They are generally fit and work out 2–3 times a week.
	• Buy their produce from XYZ store because it is organic and healthy.

The intention of this comparison is not to completely invalidate market segments, but to emphasize the difference and the need to have both. Customer personas are born out of market segments. Market segmentation is the basic function of any marketing function, and accordingly, the author assumes that this segmentation is already achieved in the business.

The comparison poses an interesting question: which is easier to sell to, focusing only on market segments or customer persona Jane? Which would the sales team be better prepared to deal with? Whose needs would the customer service team be able to address better?

Customer personas help the business better understand who it is dealing with and how it can add value to them. Remember the *V1C?* It must match exactly the customer persona.

Now customer personas may seem difficult to develop, but they are actually not, if done right. So here is your guide to developing customer personas, which consists of these steps:

Step 1: Setup
As in any project, the planning or setup phase is the most critical. In it, the boundaries are set, resources allocated, and expectations/outcomes clarified, that is, if a positive outcome is desired. Embarking on discovering customer personas is no different.

During this step, there are three matters that need to be addressed: a) Team, b) Scope, and C) Quantity.

Team

Developing customer personas cannot and should not be the sole responsibility of the sales team and should not be carried out behind closed doors. Equally important, it cannot be based on intuitions. This is a data-driven exercise and involves the entire company. The whole company needs to be educated on the customer personas because it will affect every aspect of their role and how they interact with customers. The team in charge of developing the customer personas must consist of people from different disciplines within the business. This may vary based on the organization structure and how business is conducted, but it should include the following representatives from at least these functions:

1. Senior management: Provide direction
2. Sales: Customer needs
3. Customer service: Feedback on problems faced by customers
4. Marketing: Market and customer data
5. Finance and IT: Data and analytics
6. Operations   Viability and/or process changes

Be mindful not to create large teams. They tend to complicate more than solve; a well-selected few can do a tremendous job.

Scope

A crucial yet often-overlooked step is refining the existing customer to fit the newly revised Value-to-Customer *(VtC) or* designing a whole set of new customer segment to fit into the new *VtC*. This distinction is critical, as it gives the team the focus, in addition to saving you money. Yes, savings!

Enhancing existing customers is cheaper because of data previously available from interactions with existing customers, CRM databases, financial and sales reports, and so on. Contrarily, preparing personas for future customers presents challenges in obtaining data and speaking to potential customers. So, it is critical to clarify from the onset which option are you taking.

One other major drawback is that the team may struggle to decide on which personas to work on, disturbing team cohesion, as some will want to focus on the new and others on the old.

Quantity

How many personas should be developed? Should one customer persona be created for each market segment? Before answering these key questions, it would be helpful to distinguish the difference between segments and personas and, more importantly, emphasize what the persona represents.

There are four types of customer personas:

Persona Name	Nature	Description
1. Current Customer	Positive	Who are our customers today?
2. Future Customer	Positive	Who are the customers that we want to target that we are not currently addressing?
3. Content Audience	Positive	Potential customers that consume information for educational or knowledge reasons. They could become customers in future.
4. Not Customers	Negative	Negative personas, however, are the customer personas that you don't want. In strategy and guiding a business, clarity on what you don't want is of more importance. Imagine the efficiency of the sales process when the sales team is completely clear on the customer they should and should not pursue. How much time and money would be saved?!

There is no clear science to determine the number of which ones should be prepared and how many in each category, but to start, aim not to exceed four and go from there.

Step 2: Gather Data

Data for developing customer personas can be obtained from a few sources, but is mostly based on how you run your business, i.e. web-based, CRM, etc.:

1. Talking with Customers
2. Online interactions
3. CRM
4. Surveys
5. Google analytics and AdWords
6. Etc.

Hands down, the most reliable source of information is to speak directly to customers, and preferably not through a survey company, but via the team itself. The team should develop a set of questions to ask each customer, present, future or both, and gather that information into Customer Persona Profiles.

Sample Questions

These are sample questions to get you started:

1. Gather personal demographics:
    - Gender, age, marital status, number of children and their ages, address, educational background, field of business, job role or title
    - Other relevant information required by the business
2. Which publications or blogs do you read?
3. Which associations or social networks do you participate in?
4. What are the skills required to do your job?
5. What tools do you use?

6. Do you prefer texting or calling?
7. Order online or by phone?
8. How are you measured for success?
9. What does a typical day look like?
10. How do you learn about new information in your job? Personal life?
11. How do you prefer to interact with vendors?
12. How do you search for information?
13. Describe a recent purchase.
14. Do you prefer online shopping and why?
15. Why do you like our product or service?
16. What don't you like about our product or service? Why?
17. Have you tried a competing product? What did you like about it?
18. What would you like to see change in our product or service?
19. What are some of the challenges that you regularly face?
20. Do you prefer farmers' markets or supermarkets and why?
21. What would make your day?
22. If you could imagine three products that would solve your most pressing problem, what would they be?

Sample Customer Persona Profile Template

There is no good or bad template; there is only what works for your business. The following is just an example and can be modified to whatever suits the business.

Persona Name:	**Coupon Ben**
Attribute	*Description*
Background and Demographics	• First job at a bank • Working for 2 years • Male, age 24 • Single • Girlfriend
Communication Preferences	• Prefers online purchases than going to store • Email instead of calls • Do-it-yourself

Persona Name:	**Coupon Ben**
Defines Success as	• Leaving at 5:00 p.m. sharp with no pending to-dos for tomorrow
Challenges	• Financial constraints: Making ends meet • Getting things done on time, reports to 2 people.
Interesting Quotes	• "I can't be bothered to talk to customer service."
Leisure time	• Reading • Playing and watching basketball
Goals	• Aspiration to start own business in a few years

Other Data

As mentioned earlier, there are numerous sources of data, so it would strengthen the customer personas if they are supported by data from actual sales and CRM systems, as well as visits to websites and SEO (Search Engine Optimization) analysis, that is already provided through online tools like Google Analytics and AdWords.

STEP 3: BUILD PERSONAS

The final step, we are almost there. Now that we have the data, templates, and surveys all lined up, the next task is to sort through all this information and determine the characteristics of our ideal customers. There are free online tools to help you build your personas like: https://uxpressia. com/personas-online-tool or https://www.vbout.com/buyer-persona.

Unfortunately, there is no formula for "how to put the data together." It is an art form to design the right customer persona. But it is an art form that starts easily and simply and grows with time. So, do not be disappointed; start simple and grow your personas. They will not be perfect the first time and will probably take a few iterations before reaching the level you desire. But it is worth it as it positively impacts sales and focuses your marketing efforts.

Repeat Regularly

Customer personas change similarly to how people change. There are certain things that we keep constant; others change with time.. As such, it's not acceptable to consider that the customer personas are static and last for years without any change. Technology is changing, and it is impacting the buying habits of people along with it.

For the business to stay on top of these changes and stay relevant to their customers, the personas need to be updated regularly. Given this reality, this process should be done at least 2–4 times per year, or better yet, as a continuous stream. Meaning, customer meetings should be happening constantly throughout the year, and the feedback is to be reported back into the templates and shared with the business.

9 Deadly Sins of Customer Personas

Sin	Description
1. How Many…?	Having too many personas will most probably backfire on the business. This translates to overlapping personas and no clear differences between the personas, leading to confusion and mistakes in dealing with the customer.
2. Only the Positive Prevail	It is important to define the positive personas as well as the negative ones. Don't brush this off. The negatives help us understand the positive personas even better.
3. Personas, a Marketing Tool	Customer personas are not just a marketing tool. Their effect should be prevalent across the business. Example: if most of the customers prefer dealing with emails and online, then why would you invest heavily in a call center?
4. Personas for Life	Personas are not a once-in-a-lifetime deal to be developed once and forgotten for a few years. That's one of the reasons why most SMBs don't last for long. Personas change regularly, and it is important to update them 2–3 times a year. That's the way to stay ahead of the curve and detect disruptors swiftly.

Sin	Description
5. My Friend, Mr. Persona	Personas are generalizations and should not be reflective of an individual person. Instead, they should be a grouping of ideal customers' characteristics. So, to drive the message home, instead of calling it John or Mary, try John Single Dad or Marketing Mary.
6. It's Absolutely Aspirational	Beware of distinguishing between your current and future customer personas and make everyone understand the difference. It is important to be clear on both. Failing to do so might get your team confused and waste valuable resources perusing the wrong persona.
7. Just Use Google	While Google is a life saver with all the tools and analyses it provides, solely basing your personas on Google searches will be disastrous. You must go out and speak to your customers; there is nothing more valuable than that.
8. Customers Would Meet with Us for Free	No, they won't! If you want to have valuable information from your customers and get them to spend valuable time explaining various aspects of their lives, you need to make it worth their while, and don't be cheap. Let them feel that they are valuable to you; they will become customers for life.
9. It Costs Too Much	No, it does not! This is a mission critical function, and it will cost more, in lost sales and suffering disruptors, to not get personas right. Competition is increasing and if your business does not understand who it is selling to, it will soon be forgotten.

<u>CONTENT</u>

Don't you find it funny that almost every hotel website is pretty much the same design? Pictures of the rooms and a widget to help you book for specific dates. One could even argue that this is what you should expect from a hotel.

However, if we were to take a look at the website from the perspective of customer personas, this assumption would not apply. That is to say, if the ideal customer was a business traveler then showing how the hotel caters to the business traveler would prove to be more effective, such as displaying the location, its ample transportation to business hubs, quick check-in and check-out process, designated work spaces in the room, etc. In contrast, if the ideal customer was on a family vacation, the first thing the customer should see is all the fun activities that can be arranged, the food options, how they cater to children of different ages. What do you think? Wouldn't that hotel stand out from the rest and achieve higher sales?

Content is a powerful form of marketing, to the point that Seth Godin said, "Content marketing is the only marketing left." Officially described, content marketing is a type of marketing that involves the creation and sharing of online material (such as videos, blogs, and social media posts), which does not explicitly promote a brand, but is intended to stimulate interest in its products or services.

Why is it important? Well...

1. Traditional marketing is losing its appeal. Customer purchasing habits have changed, and they want to be informed before they buy. Reflect on your own likelihood of reaching for customer reviews prior to both your minor or major purchases. Now factor in the impact of the Internet, and users no longer need a screen to digest content.

2. Trust, credibility, and transparency. Customers, regardless of their generation, want to know the good, the bad, and the ugly about your product or service. So, you can choose to be at the mercy and whims of social media users or tackle this head-on. Produce content that is relevant to your customers, with authenticity and integrity, while remaining engaging throughout.

3. Credibility! Content is a way for your business to demonstrate its credibility and be an authority on the product or service being sold.

Content creation may seem like a daunting task, but as with all things, having the right strategy, process and people behind it, it becomes part of the daily business. You must first accept that content marketing should be a major part of your marketing. Period. Now let's talk about the key elements to produce it.

Elements of Content Marketing

A successful content marketing function has, at its foundation, a deep understanding of the customer segments being targeted, i.e. customer personas. Good news! You already have them. Now it comes down to:

1. *Content Strategy:*
   The content strategy is a short document to keep you on the path. Like anything in life or in business, you always need to be clear on what you are trying to do and how. A content strategy is no exception. You already know your value-add to the customer (*VtC*) and who your ideal customers are; now all you need to figure out is what information they need in order to choose to buy your product or service. This information must be free, unbiased, authentic, and generous.

2. *Content Calendar:*
   Based on your strategy, you must have a calendar. This calendar will organize you and set some expectations from your customers.

3. *Metrics:*
   Measurement is key. You will be gauging the success of your content strategy by seeing how it is translating into visits, customer inquiries, sales dollars, etc. But you also need to put relevant metrics in place to measure.

The three elements above are highly unique to each business. It is impractical to believe that they can be copied from another business. This is where your business will shine in its own unique way. Become a leader of your industry in providing your customers with all the information they need, upfront and free. You earn their trust, their appreciation, and you are set up for success.

PROCESS

Customer personas are a great place to kick off, to focus the business, and to begin the journey of breaking the ceiling that's been holding you and your business back. Defining the personas is the straightforward part. For the change to start, the impact of the personas and *VtC* must permeate throughout the business. This is doubtlessly going to be the hardest part. Why? Because it is where you and your business will need to get out of the comfort zone and move into unchartered waters. In other words, it's the true test of your customer personas and *VtC*.

To support us on this change journey, we will need to look at the business from a perspective different from what is traditionally known. Think of your business as these functions:

1. Product or service delivery functions
2. Customer support functions
3. Business support functions

The purpose of this section is to provide a guide to determine the changes needed in your business. However, you'll find this process is unique to each company and its leader. As such, the guide presents a set of actions and underlying principles to guide you through this journey.

Product/Service Delivery Functions

	Description	*Example*
What are these functions?	These are the functions that are directly responsible for delivering the goods or services to the customers; e.g. operations, sales, etc.	In retail, the salesperson on the showroom floor. In manufacturing, the salesperson meeting customers and responding to requests for quotes. In services, the customer service rep that books the sale or the online process for sales.
Guiding principles	The *VtC* sums up what we are to our customers.	Fast, efficient, easy alternative
How to change	Map out the key processes that deal with customers and for each process ask these questions:	Key processes are site inspection by survey team, quote preparation by sales team, and installation by technicians.
	1. Does this process represent our *VtC*? If yes, how does it fit into our *VtC*? If no, what needs to change for it to fit?	No, it takes 3–5 days from receiving the customer call to providing the customer with a quote and 2–3 days from customer acceptance to installing the product.
	2. If changes are needed, how will we measure whether the changes are working or not? What kind of metrics should we use?	Our response time from initial customer call to installation should not be more than 3 days.
	3. Do the changes require skillsets that we do not currently have within the team? If yes, what are they and what is required to upskill our team members?	Yes, we need to train our surveyors to provide quotes on the spot. They can be trained to do that for $500 per person; complete team could be trained within 2 weeks. They will be supported by a pricing guide from the sales team.

	Description	*Example*
	4. Do we need additional capital expenditure to implement the changes, e.g. new machinery, upgrades, etc.? If yes, how much and where do we get the money from?	Yes, surveyors need laptops to be able to input the information and email customers a quote on the spot. Each laptop is $900. A total of 20 are required. Funds can be reallocated from the business travel budget and by making redundant 2 salespersons, who currently handle the quotations.
	5. Will these changes increase our operating cost? If yes, by how much? Can anything be done to reduce the impact of cost increase?	No, they would actually reduce operating costs by 9%.
Potential challenges	What are the challenges or difficulties we might face in implementing the changes and how will they be handled?	• Challenge: Resistance to change, some surveyors may not feel comfortable issuing quotes. • Challenge: Sales team would be in an uproar for redundancies within their department • Solution: The change program needs to be communicated to the team in an honest and transparent manner and that it is for the good of the company. Unfortunately, some changes are required.

Customer Support Functions

	Description	*Example*
What are these functions?	These are the functions that are directly responsible for interacting with the customers after the sale is completed.	Mainly customer service and call centers
Guiding principles	The *VtC* sums up what we are to our customers.	Fast, efficient, easy alternative
How to change	Map out the key processes that deal with customers and for each process ask these questions:	Key processes are receiving customer call or complaint, acknowledging receipt of complaint, and acting to resolve complaint.
	1. Do these processes represent our *VtC*? If yes, how do they fit into our *VtC*? If no, what needs to change for them to fit.	No, on average, the customer is on hold for 10 minutes before we can speak to them. We need to reduce that time to answering our customer on the third ring and within 1 minute on social media.
	2. If changes are needed, how will we measure whether the changes are working or not? What kind of metrics should we use?	The key metrics for measuring success are: • Average speed to speak to customer • Average time to resolve customer problem
	3. Do the changes require skill-sets that we do not currently have within the team? If yes, what are they and what is required to upskill our team members?	No, our customer support staff are well trained in dealing with customer complaints; our problem is in the speed to respond.

	Description	*Example*
	4. Do we need additional capital expenditure to implement the changes, e.g. new machinery, upgrades, etc.? If yes, how much and where do we get the money from?	Yes, a new customer relationship system, as well as a call management system, is required. Also, additional staff hires are needed, especially in our social media team. Capital expenses of $75,000. Funds will be allocated from the budget contingency.
	5. Will these changes increase our operating cost? If yes, by how much? Can anything be done to reduce the impact of cost increase? Is a price increase required?	Yes, will need to hire 3 more people to handle the increasing workload. Average annual cost increase is $80,000. Will have a 0.85% reduction in profit margin.
Potential challenges	What are the challenges or difficulties we might face in implementing the changes and how will they be handled?	• Challenge: Procurement and implementation of the new systems will require 3–5 months. • Solution: Apply tight project management controls over the implementation to ensure that it does not slip. Weekly report to senior management on progress.

Business Support Functions

	Description	Example
What are these functions?	These are the functions that are directly responsible for supporting the business in fulfilling its *VtC*.	Finance, IT, and procurement
Guiding principles	The *VtC* sums up what we are to our customers.	Fast, efficient, easy alternative
How to change	Map out the key processes that deal with customers and for each process ask these questions:	Financial reporting Maintenance of systems Efficient and timely logistics
	1. Do these processes represent our *VtC*? If yes, how do they fit into our *VtC*? If no, what needs to change for them to fit?	Our financial reports are issued in the third week of the month, which is a long time to wait to assess the results of the month. We do not have daily or weekly reports.
	2. If changes are needed, how will we measure whether the changes are working or not? What kind of metrics should we use?	Daily sales reports by following morning and month-end reports ready within 4 days of closing.
	3. Do the changes require skillsets that we do not currently have within the team? If yes, what are they and what is required to upskill our team members?	Yes, Finance is understaffed and doesn't have senior-level resources to guide the team. CFO to be hired.

	Description	*Example*
	4. Do we need additional capital expenditure to implement the changes, e.g. new machinery, upgrades, etc.? If yes, how much and where do we get the money from?	Yes, some system enhancements are required costing $15,000 and would need 4 weeks to implement.
	5. Will these changes increase our operating cost? If yes, by how much? Can anything be done to reduce the impact of cost increase? Is a price increase required?	Yes, new CFO position cost will need to be absorbed, approx. $95,000.
Potential challenges	What are the challenges or difficulties we might face in implementing the changes and how will they be handled?	• Challenge: Function has been running with skeleton staff, and a new CFO would disturb the status quo; some employees may feel threatened and leave. • Solution: risk that we will need to manage through honest and transparent communication

Data and Update

Throughout this process, it is critical that data is collected and analyzed continuously. The data will let us know whether or not our assumptions about the personas and subsequent changes to the business are producing the required results. It's imperative to realize that you will not get it right from the first round; this is an iterative process that requires constant and unrelenting adjustment and improvement. We do not live in a static world. Our best defense to its consistent and rapid changing is constant measurement and adjustment of our course of action.

DISRUPTORS

It seems that every other company these days has the objective of disrupting some industry or another. I find this particularly interesting and wonder, Did the companies that we call disruptors really set out to disrupt an industry from the start? Let me answer that by recalling an interview with one of the founders of Airbnb, a true disruptor in their own right. When they launched the company, their goal was never to disrupt, but to add value. They started the company and failed 5 times before it became a success. They succeeded because they sought to create value and not solely disrupt. That is an ever-so-important distinction. When you set your sights on being a company of value, then yes, you will disrupt those who took their position for granted and didn't listen to their customers; those who allowed for the gaps in the market to happen didn't heed the changing dynamics in customer preferences and needs.

My point is not to burden the business with trying to figure out where the next disruption is coming from, but to encourage you stay close to the customer and better understand them. Then the changes in their preferences will be clear and will direct you to make corresponding changes to your business in such a way that a disruptor cannot find value to add to your customers who you take care of ever so diligently.

Another point to emphasize is that to protect against disruptions a company must do 2 things: 1) stay close to the customer, as previously mentioned, and 2) to innovate, a topic we will discuss in the chapter titled "Unleashing Creative Genius."

UNLEASHING CREATIVE GENIUS— *INNOVATION*

Business has only two functions—marketing and innovation.

—Peter Drucker

Life is ever changing, and change can go both ways: either up or down, growth or decline. With innovation, the chances of growth are much higher, whereas if you stay constant and produce the same level of products or services, without improvement, i.e. change, your business will start to decline and eventually fade away, as we had discussed in our earlier chapter on business life cycles.

At the core, innovation is the one thing that will save your business from dying. Naturally, there are multiple other issues that may harm your business, but if you have a solid running business that is profitable, with cash flows and good quality products, the one thing that can hurt your business is proceeding without innovation.

Innovation is linked to the survival of the organization. This chapter discusses some of the common mistakes as well as valuable practices of how to build that innovation and integrate it into your culture moving forward. Prior to beginning, we need to identify and define innovation.

What is Innovation?

If you speak to 10 separate business leaders about innovation, you will get 10 different answers. The best I have come across was a definition developed by Nick Skillicorn, chief editor and founder of *Idea to Value*. Nick surveyed 15 innovation practitioners and collected their thoughts on what is beneficial and what is detrimental and from that produced the following definition of innovation:

> ***It is executing an idea which addresses a specific challenge and achieves value for both the company and the customer.***
>
> **—Nick Skillicorn**

This definition entirely captures the essence of innovation in that:

1. It is not only about identifying ideas, but executing them.
2. It must address a specific challenge.
3. It needs to add value for both the company and the customer.

Innovation and Business Knowledge

There's a very important link between business knowledge, i.e. knowledge of how the business is running, and innovation. This link is often overlooked due to the overhype associated with the concept of innovation in business.

Often a business seeking to innovate would hire a new team to handle the innovation, in an attempt to inject some fresh blood into the business, or hire a consultant to help them go through the process of innovation. However, this begins to fail if the senior leadership doesn't realize that true innovation is actually *delivering* on new products or services or gathering of ideas, rather than focusing on only coming up with those ideas. To deliver, the innovation team needs someone who can translate those ideas into implementable steps that fit within the organization's business model and, more importantly, its culture! This is the stage where business knowledge is critical.

So, coming up with a bunch of ideas is one thing, but translating those ideas into reality is another. To be able to address this challenge, careful consideration should be given to the team that is leading the innovation initiative. They should reflect a healthy mix of old and new, process and design, vision and mechanics.

It is essential to understand that there's a full execution cycle from identification to execution, and the importance of how the business works into this equation cannot be.

Common Mistakes of Innovation

1. *Not Enough Resources (Time, Money, People, and Culture)*
   When a company talks about having innovation as part of its values, and doesn't back it up with enough support to execute, that destroys any innovation culture they are trying to achieve. The failure stems from not providing the required level of time and budget to take these ideas, refine them, experiment with them, and finally turn them into an applicable solution.

2. *Innovating the Product Instead of the Business*
   Part of developing a valuable product is instilling improvements into the core process of the business. By introducing a certain technology or improving the technology within the process, or building or manufacturing the product, you allow better-quality production in the end. This also applies in terms of service. If you provide additional tools to your team, then the quality of service

improves, or you can recover your costs to become more competitive. Although you can go both ways, the improvement *has* to come from within the business for it to manifest itself to your customers.

3. *Managing the Volume of Ideas*

When businesses ask for ideas, especially from the public, the volume of ideas flowing back can become distractions if not managed properly. This volume should not be viewed as detrimental and may include some profitable ideas.

To manage the volume, and reduce the noise and distractions to a controllable level, the business should be armed with a clear set of guidelines on what it is looking for and what is considered acceptable. It must then be regimented in applying those guidelines.

An organization can implode from the weight of all these ideas, and the noise they generate can get overwhelming and distract from the ultimate Destination.

4. *Disruption vs. Value-add*

When a business starts to focus on seeking the next disruptive idea, that in itself is a damaging goal! A lot of companies are going around saying, "We are working on the next disruptive technology" or "We seek to disrupt this or that industry."

A lot of the businesses that are disruptive in their own right did not start off by stating that they wanted to disrupt an industry; think Uber and Airbnb, etc. They started by focusing on adding value. They identified the gap in the market and went after it, creating value for their customers.

If we *focus* on disruption itself, this negative emotion approach does not generate the right attitude. The right attitude is to aim to generate value. By generating perceptible value-add, the business will cause disruption. And that's how you produce a disruptive idea—not by labelling it a disruptive idea, just to fulfil your aim. It needs to add value!

5.   *The Language Used*
A business needs to be cautious with the language it uses to describe ideas or initiatives. When you label ideas as breakthroughs, regardless of their impact and size, you're actually lowering the bar and, in a way, allowing for mediocrity to settle in.

So, if it's a breakthrough, call it a breakthrough. But if it's an idea, call it an idea. I know these are semantics, but language does matter in terms of how it focuses people and gets them to appreciate progress. So, if every single idea generated is labelled as awesome, then "awesome" ceases to have any value. Be particularly mindful of the type of language you attach to the idea generation process specifically and the innovation process as a whole generally.

6.   *Lack of Focus*
When a business has an unfocused conversation about innovation, then the frame is set too wide to result in a meaningful impact. Any idea would pretty much hit the mark. Or if the frame is set too narrow, you're boxing yourself into constraints that would leave the problem unsolved or, at best, artificially addressed. Be precise and focused on what problem you are trying to address.

Unfortunately, what happens a lot in these cases is that a senior leader within the business needs a new idea fast, so they start pushing everybody to come up with new ideas and will use awful overused terms like "think outside the box," "paradigm shift," "breakdown the silos," and so on. I am begging all such business leaders, please throw all those clichés out and ask the simple direct question, "What is the problem that we are trying to solve?" and then let your people get creative about how to solve it.

7. *Unclear Process for Innovation*

A common error when launching innovation is to send people into a room and ask them to come up with a bunch of ideas. What happens after they come back with ideas? How do we take an idea, map it out, test it, see if it works, and then develop the product or service and sell it to customers? If that process is unclear, you'll find people stumbling and unsure of their next task. It becomes a best-guess scenario, which will result in additional costs and inefficiencies for you.

8. *Neglecting the Basics of Business*

Business is an intellectual sport, and I believe we need to heed that statement. Coming up with grand ideas, then throwing the basics of business to the wind, will result in a very expensive mistake.

Part of the innovation process should include a business viability assessment. Questions like: How much money is required to make this happen? What will the returns be and over what period? What is the free cash flow being generated? Is this idea sustainable? What is the size of the market? Go through what you consider business basics before implementing an idea. Not only have we come up with a worthy idea, let us implement it and take it through the motions.

9. *Punishing People for Experimenting*

This is probably one of the biggest detriments to your innovation culture: if somebody makes a mistake and they are punished, this alerts everyone else in the business to stick to their status quo and refrain from coming up with anything new, because its failure will result in their punishment.

That approach is destructive and contrary to what the business needs. Instead, the situation should be analyzed with this person and walked through what happened, to identify what was done well and what were the lessons learned, then kept in a log with general access granted to all. At the beginning of that log, write the following statement: "We stand on the shoulders of those before us; make your mark here!" By celebrating failures, you are allowing others to step in and experiment; that's how your team become masters and your business flourishes.

Good Practices in Innovation

1. Framing the challenge correctly is a critical key to innovation. There is no way around that. You need to be clear about what the challenge is.

2. Change the conversation within the organization. Instead of having it as a small group, or one or two isolated people, bring the dialogue into the organization by asking inclusive questions like: *How can we make this better? How can we test it? How can we implement it? How can we get closer to our customers?* Once you're engaging in all aspects of the organization, within reason, this new conversation has to be managed carefully. Avoid opening the conversation to the point of being flooded with bizarre or irrelevant ideas that will bog you down. It's a dialogue, so have a conversation with your customers. That's the best way to get sources of information, as we've discussed in the section on identifying customer personas.

3. For the most effective results, focus on the question, not the solution. Avoid the tyranny of "how."

4. Listening more to your customers. A high level of engagement with your customers on a constant basis will allow the business to better understand what the pain points of customers are. These pain points are the clearest signs of where you need to focus the innovation efforts.

5. Make long-term investments in innovation culture, and do not approach this culture from a one-off project perspective. For example, sales are down, so it is decided that there needs to be some focus on innovation. Resources are allocated, and ideas are generated; it works! And sales are up again. Don't allow your business to forget about innovation until the next time sales take a dip. You need to continuously feed the innovation machine and make sure there is a constant flow of resources available for this machine throughout the year.

6. Don't accept the status quo. Refuse it. It can always be better; it can always be different; it can always be approved.

7. Set clear and simple goals. For example, at least one new product every year. That's a target that everybody can understand, everybody can focus on, everybody can work with.

    But critical to this is to ensure that these objectives are backed up with tangible actions. Continuing with the example of one new product a year, should the business deliver on that, there needs to be a supporting reward system. It can't be just talk.

8. Innovation needs to be integrated into the organizational thinking of the business, so when you are having separate conversations about production issues or finance, or reports and so on, innovation needs to be embedded within each. It's not a one-off project; it's a conversation that needs to continue throughout the business and needs to refer back to Peter Drucker's opening quote, "Innovation and marketing are the two things that business should focus on." Always keep that at the forefront of your approach.

9. Keep in mind that you need to move from idea generation to product commercialization. Many organizations adhere too strictly to

a process and forget that innovation means taking an idea and executing it successfully.

10. You need to ensure there is diversity in your innovation team. Having either exclusively junior people or senior people will skew their process and outcome. This approach is a practice of Procter & Gamble. Whenever they have a new product, they work to place a senior, with years of experience, with someone who is relatively junior, possessing fresh ambition and excitement. Make sure that there's a healthy mix of men and women on the team. Research has proven that incorporating women into the team improves your chances of success. Finally, involve employees of different cultural backgrounds to address challenges. Aim to always have these 3 factors of diversity in place.

11. Executive support must be visible, in that the executives must be supportive of hosting internal events, like workshops or boot camps. The executives need to show face and say, yes, we are behind this and putting their money where their mouth is. Not doing so, again, will backfire on this innovation culture.

The Cost of Innovation
How much money should be allocated to innovation?

The cost of innovation is a trigger question. But a more perceptive question would be, "Can the business afford not to innovate?" The reality is that refusing to innovate will cause your business to decline and eventually fade away.

Investment in innovation does not need to consume a large portion of your profits. Instead, view it as a business necessity and allocate the required funds to it. There are various options that do not require copious amounts of resources but rather different thinking. For example, giving people the time to work on a project of their choice or set up competitions. There are several ways you can utilize the resources that you currently possess internally, without necessarily having to vastly invest on an innovation project.

Cost of innovation could also be viewed as a form of capital expenditure that has a useful life and should be replaced after a period of time, similar concept to depreciation. Innovation should have an annual allocation of funds to support it. It must be part of the annual budget.

Next Steps

Consider implementing these eight steps for a healthy innovation culture.

1. **Commitment:** There has to be an allocation of time, budget, and executive time for your innovation team.

2. **Team:** Make sure that the team is diversified, knowledgeable, experienced, and understands the question.

3. **Focus:** Identify what the customer issues are or the problem within the organization that you're trying to innovate for.

4. **Risk:** Realize that risk is part of innovation, so you cannot innovate without taking risks, and this must be accepted. However, the degree of this risk is a different story. You need to understand that.

5. **Coaching:** The executives have to coach the innovation team and the organization on the importance of innovation and how to tackle and solve problems.

6. **Process:** There has to be a clear path from idea to commercialization. People need to understand what that process is and follow it.

7. **Measure:** This may be the most significant point. You must keep track of what works and what doesn't and keep it in a log, accessible to everyone. How much money is being spent and where? You

have to find and measure the success of a certain approach you've taken. Measurement is key for sustaining innovation.

8. **Reward:** It must match the objectives or the solutions identified. I'm not saying we need to solely reward financially, based on the results. We've shown scientifically that doesn't work. But we need to design a reward scheme that appreciates people's efforts accordingly.

Afterthought

Innovation requires alternative approaches to imbed it into the business and integrate it into the daily operations. It is a challenge to be undertaken and cannot happen overnight.

Challenges will be faced when pulling people from delivering the product or service to work on an innovation project or when allocating funds to innovation projects that could otherwise be used in another part of the business. And despite that, I stress its importance.

Work on maintaining your optimal balance in the face of these challenges. The survival of your business depends on it!

ENGAGING YOUR TEAM—
EMPLOYEES

To win in the marketplace,
you must first win in the workplace.

—*Doug Connent, CEO of Campbell's Soup*

No matter the business size, its people persist to be its backbone. There is an ample amount of research on how to motivate employees, better understand their needs, the mindset of different generations X, Y, millennials. The research is endless and will remain so, while, though much has been uncovered, much more remains unclear. One thing is certain, no business can exist without its team.

A compelling area of research is on the varied approach associated with the diverse generations in the workplace. If you take a moment to contemplate the multi-generational differences in the workplace, from a perspective of the basic needs of humans, you may agree that regardless of the generation, there are several similarities between them. We, as people, require safety; we need to belong, we need to explore, we need to grow. The minute we realize that, at the core, we are more similar than we are different, it paints a very altered picture on how we engage with our teams.

This chapter is about exploring how to better engage the backbone of any business—its people! For SMBs, engaging the team has a more profound impact due to their size and an even higher impact if they don't get it right. Key challenges SMBs face when it comes to engaging their teams are:

1.   It's hard to find talented resources.
2.   It's hard to motivate them.
3.   They are fickle and don't see the big picture.
4.   There's a lack of commitment.

This list serves to highlight that the challenges are symptoms, and not the root cause of employee disengagement. This chapter takes a fresh look at employee-related matters and aims to subdue these symptoms by addressing the root cause of the problems, to bring a noticeable improvement in employee engagement.

1. Attitude Reflects Leadership

A common complaint amongst business owners is that their employees don't always follow requests as prescribed, choosing instead to carry out alternate tasks than what they were told. It's frustrating, and more dangerously, it's costing the business owner money in wasted efficiency and/or in correcting errors.

There are two reasons for that. One is capabilities. Either the person cannot or does not have the capabilities to carry out the task at hand. That is easily addressable through either training or replacement. These are your only options if it's a capability issue.

Then there's attitude. It's not the attitude of the employee that is worrisome; it's actually the attitude of leadership. Because the attitude of the employee is a reflection of the leadership, and it's *your* leadership, as the business owner.

A study was published in the Harvard Business Review by Daniel Goldman and Richard Boyatzis titled, "Social Intelligence and the Biology of Leadership." The authors present the research on how the mood of the leader will ripple throughout the organization. Regardless of size, the ripple will go through the organization. They called it "mood contagion." If the leader of the business walks into the office and has a smile on their face, greets people with "good morning" and a cheerful attitude, that resonates and triggers certain neurons in the brain that causes people to begin mimicking this behavior.

Similarly, if the leader of the business walks in with a frown on their face, starts shouting and berating people and openly displays their internal frustration, it reflects throughout the entire business. Scientific research showed that it's linked to chemicals in the brain being released.

So, the statement "attitude reflects leadership" is in the literal sense!

I encourage you to examine your attitude in the workplace. Consider how you are in these scenarios:

- Are you the person that shows up on time or is always late for meetings?
- How do you conduct meetings? Are you focused, have an agenda prepared, or do you use meetings to catch up on market gossip?
- How do you speak to your team? Is it by barking orders or in a constructive manner?
- How much pressure do you apply on your team? Is it always pressure, pressure, pressure, "it's urgent and required tomorrow," or do you actively manage stress levels?

You'll find that all these behaviors reflect your attitude to the people running your business. Punctuality shows respect, focus shows strong leadership and control, speaking with respect reflects compassion, managing stress levels shows a leader who will not lose control at the first challenge. Attitude directly reflects leadership!

Below are examples from my own personal experience emphasizing how "attitude reflects leadership."

1. At a firm I previously worked, semi-annual regional meetings were held to discuss performance and tackle any issues impeding our growth. As one of the newest members of the team, I arrived at the meeting site at 8:20 a.m., only 10 minutes before the meeting was due to start. I found nobody else there. At first, I thought I had the wrong address and panicked. Reassured by the sign at the door, I waited, until slowly, around 9:00 a.m., people started showing up. Finally, our leader arrived at 10:30 a.m., and sat for a quick bite before commencing the 2-day long meeting.

    The remaining days proceeded in the same manner—frankly, as a complete waste of time with no focused agenda and constant avoidance of every pressing question. A horrible first experience, the message was loud and clear: none of us are seen as valuable, the leader will do as he pleases, and don't bother asking any questions. I left the firm shortly thereafter. Classic example of a senseless waste of resources.

    It's an extreme case, but it's one to consider. Being 10–15 minutes late is 10–15 minutes wasted by all attending that meeting, which could have been utilized to take care of their job and earnings.

2. Another example is of weekly status meetings, which are of importance if run correctly and efficiently. A company I knew had a leader who loved the weekly status meetings and usually had them held in the afternoon to minimize the impact on the day's productivity. Starting around 3:00 p.m. and lasting for a minimum of 3 hours. However, throughout these meetings, several attendees

would take the floor only to reminisce about their achievements and what they've been trying to do. There was no clear structure and very little productive outcome. This largely useless weekly time investment can be very frustrating and wasteful.

The message relayed to the employees is the leader has no appreciation for our time or theirs. Since it's a culture of waste, then employees feel validated to reciprocate and show up late or miss a few deadlines.

These are all indicators. As the business leader, assess whether you are indulging in these habits and how it eventually impacts your business. Any direct impact on employee morale is a direct impact on cash flow.

2) Intrinsic vs. Extrinsic Motivators

A quote by Dan Ariely, from the 2009 *New York Times* article, based on research carried out in multiple countries, *"We found that as long as the task involved only mechanical skill, bonuses worked as would be expected. The higher the pay, the better the performance. But when we included a task that required even rudimentary cognitive skill, the offer of a higher bonus led to poorer performance."*

That is a shockingly different approach from what business practices are today!

The research is confirming that the more money you give people, the worse they perform on the job. What's interesting about this research is that it's not uniquely set to a certain geography or culture; it was performed in poor and rich countries, all around the world, and they came in with the same results, time and time again.

The science is evident. Extrinsic motivators end up hurting your business in the long run as opposed to intrinsic motivators. To clarify, extrinsic motivators are things like money, house, cars, and so on. Intrinsic motivators are of three types: autonomy, mastery, and purpose.

1. In *autonomy*, people want to be able to work of their own accord, their own way, and not be directed on how to carry out the work.

2. With *mastery*, people want to excel at something, and to do so, you have to be allowed to fail sometimes. Unfortunately, our business culture is such that we punish failure, when we should be celebrating it, because it is failure that gets us closer to achieving success or even mastery.

3. *Purpose*. It has to hold meaning to them or their community, and only then can we motivate our team into creating that which is far beyond expectations, on a daily basis.

4. Let's examine companies like Google for instance, where they allow their engineers to take 20–40% time off, to work on personal interest projects. A lot of the products from Google actually came from those times where the engineers spent it by themselves doing what they wanted. They were motivated to create a product that held significant meaning to them; they were becoming masters at this.

A critical issue with intrinsic motivators is you can't expect employees to be intrinsically motivated or provide them with these such motivational levers, when the "basics" are not there. "Basics" include factors such as a decent working space, clean offices, and fair pay. You must provide an element of "breathing room." In SMBs, your challenge will be on how to manage expenses, but "basics" must be provided to your people, and then they can grow.

3) Resources versus Resourcefulness
Amongst the issues faced by SMBs is the need to hire people. But they can't, because of the cost constraints and so on. Sometimes the solution is not in hiring more people, but instead, looking at the problem in a more efficient way.

To do this, you must assess how a certain job can be carried out faster and better. There is a multitude of free apps that can be used to make the process more efficient or to better time manage or to talk to your customers. Also, instead of hiring a full-time assistant, why not embrace technology and consider a virtual one that costs $5–10 an hour, to relieve your salespeople of the paperwork requirements? Apply these questions and approaches to alleviate the pressure on your team.

Again, it's not an issue of resources; it's resourcefulness! Be progressively resourceful and implement change.

4) Change the Recruitment Process
Does it seem logical that the recruitment process of a CEO and that of a junior entry position is nearly identical? Beginning with a CV or reference, followed by a standard interview process before the decision to hire is made and that person is expected to begin their position.

Instead, I propose that you identify the deliverables and matching skill set required of the person filling this position to deliver on these requirements. Change your perspective. First, work to understand what is expected from the position and clearly define the deliverables the position holder should produce. Second, be clear about how they link to the strategic objectives of your organization.

If we consider every job as having to provide deliverables that impact the strategic objectives of the company, then immediately understanding *what kind* of skill set you're looking for becomes a lot easier, and we are clearer about *the type of people* we want in this organization.

Then the next step is to design an interview process that actually highlights or demonstrates the skills of this person. For example, if we wanted to hire a sales agent and the skills required for the sales agent are that they are aggressive, determined, and resourceful, then you need to design an interview process that would highlight that skill set. I know of a business that carries this out exceptionally:

- First, they advertised for the position by asking interested applicants to call a number.
- Once the interested candidate called the number, they hung up on them within the first 10 seconds.
- If the candidate called again, they then hung up after exchanging only a few words, for another 3–5 times.
- If the candidate continuously called back, they'd actually invite them for an interview.
- At the interview they would be intentionally rude and push them away.
- If, and only if, the candidate called to follow up were they offered the job.

A bit extreme, nevertheless, it fit what they expected that position to deliver. The candidates demonstrated that they were aggressive, determined, and resourceful.

Let's assume you were hiring the head of procurement or looking to hire in the procurement department for a company. When they come in for an interview, instead of the traditional process of sitting and asking questions, you can alternatively put them in a mock bidding situation. Once they settle into their seats at the interview, tell them that you need their expertise in negotiating a contract next door. Put them on the spot, with little preparation, and see what they are made of. Do they excel at negotiations? Do they possess a talent for extracting information?

You will immediately be given an indication as to whether this is the right person.

Another test to use is to ask them to develop a procurement strategy for a company similar to yours and determine if they adequately understand the pitfalls or requirements of a company like yours.

Our aim is to be creative in testing if the candidate possesses the required skillsets.

Ensure that the energy of that person aligns with the values and energy levels of your business. If there is harmony amongst your team, pay careful attention to how that person's values and behaviors fit within the existing business.

Finally, make sure to give them your management-style memo and check that is something they can work with.

5) Can't Afford Top Talent

According to Jack Ma, Founder of Alibaba, "You should hire the right people and not necessarily the best people; the best people are always the ones you train." It is important that you, the business leader, are clear on what you are looking for. If you believe that a person's credentials are the only measure, you are missing some crucial elements. There is an old HR saying, "People get hired for skill set and fired for attitude." Your best people are the ones who have the skills, attitude, and passion towards the task at hand. If they have the attitude and passion, the skill can be learned. Anyone who manages people will agree that one person with a bad attitude can stifle an entire team. Yet many SMBs still see it from a talent shortage perspective. Here are a few matters to consider:

1. Be clear about the deliverables from the position that you are trying to fill. What will this position need to do to get the business to its Destination? This question, when addressed honestly, will reshape your entire approach to hiring people. It is not just about a candidate's skill set; it is also about whether they can deliver the expected outcomes of the job, within the existing cultural framework of the business.

2. What do you mean by talent? Is it an Ivy League graduate who's worked in a multinational corporation and has a stellar CV? Or are

you looking for somebody who's going to actually fit the culture and skill set, who is going to deliver on your strategic objectives?

Most would think of talent as the people who have the stellar CVs, but what you really need is the one with the skillsets who will achieve and deliver the strategic objectives and fit within your business culture. There are a few billionaires who dropped out of college: Bill Gates, Michael Dell, and Mark Zuckerberg; yet we continue to place emphasis on credentials and disregard what is required is to find the right person, possessing the right skill set, attitude and passion.

3. When you are complaining that it is tough to find "A" players, consider the question *"Is your business an A business?"*. To target the top talent, you need to be offering something attractive to them. Companies that are not "A" businesses but asking for "A" class talent is an equation that doesn't work very well.

4. Sometimes the people you need are the people you already have; they just need their skill set upgraded through training and education.

6) People Will Leave, Deal with It

Employees leaving the organization is a natural occurrence, and one that should be expected and planned for. Don't take it personally. I would like to share with you my experience with two firms, where I witnessed first-hand how they each dealt with employees leaving.

One of these firms basically celebrated the departures. If a person resigned, they would throw you a grand party, present you an expensive parting gift, and assure you that if it didn't work out at your next job you could always come back. They also created and funded an alumni network that had its own website and arranged for regular gatherings throughout the year. Simply, they made the person leaving feel special and cherished.

At the other firm, when a person resigned, it was considered an act of treason. They were looked at as unfaithful and "biting the hand that fed them." People left with a very sour taste in their mouths.

Surprisingly, both firms were in the service industry, and you can imagine who received referrals later on. Of course, it was the first firm. Whenever an alumnus needed a service, you'd go back to the old firm that took care of you and made you feel special on your way out.

People leaving is disruptive to the business, and it costs money to replace an employee, but it doesn't mean that you should punish the person who is leaving. After all, they are looking out for themselves and their families. What should upset you is if you don't have a process to identify potential backups. It doesn't have to be an elaborate succession planning exercise. Just discreetly identify the people who are suited to be potential backups for the key positions in your business.

Employees leaving can also serve as an indicator. One person leaving is the law of averages. But two people, from the same department, leaving within a short period of time is an indication of a potentially greater issue. It could also be the law of averages, but you need to examine what is taking place in that department. Is it a cultural issue? Is the manager a difficult person to work with? Is the pay insufficient? This is a prime opportunity for you to spend time and understand why your people are leaving. Not all exit interviews are 100% honest.

Part of this also relates back to the workload. A common issue with SMBs is that people are pushed hard for the most part because of lack of resources and financial constraints, trying to make ends meet, and so on. But there's a certain level of pressure where it stops making sense. If the pressure is constant, then there is a more fundamental problem with the business operating model.

Even a machine requires breaks for maintenance and repairs; now imagine a human. How long can you continue pressuring people before they start breaking down and leaving?

In the world of operations' management, if a machine is running at anything above 70% utilization, it's usually a sign of trouble. Eventually, more frequent breakdowns will occur, and the maintenance cost increases. Similarly, with people; applying constant pressure for prolonged periods will result in them breaking down and either leaving or falling ill.

But again, if you're continuously applying pressure and you don't have the financial resources to hire more people, then you have to look at the realities that a) the business model is not optimal or is broken or b) your management style is flawed or c) both.

Next Steps
Finally, there are a few things to do after going through this chapter.

1. Start taking note of how you behave at meetings, how punctual you are, how you talk, how you give instructions, how you deal with customers. As the leader, you're under the microscope, and everything you do will be magnified and replicated throughout the organization. So, you need to be aware of how you behave in all these matters because that's what is resonating with your team.

2. Understand the skills required for the key jobs in your SMB and work with your HR team to figure out a more effective interview process. Take a decision that the next hire should go through a different recruitment process. Write down and share your management style memo; it's such a powerful tool.

3. Examine your people's utilization and work to identify those who are working the hardest and how they can be given further support.

4. Keep a list of people who are potential backups for key positions.

5. Identify tasks that can be outsourced through online services or through virtual support staff and so on. It will drastically reduce costs and increase efficiency.

6. Finally, talk to your team. Understand what motivates them, see how you can give them some autonomy, mastery, and purpose. Engage them in reassuring them of your support and how you'd like to experiment with new ideas. Emphasize that it's okay if the experiments fail and that you will remain committed to your team and are invested in their well-being as well. That will have a huge impact. Give them some time to work on personal projects.

   Yes, some people might abuse this approach, but they can be weeded out. The people who will really benefit will shine. Celebrate success. More importantly, celebrate failure. Sit down; talk about failure. Create a process to identify lessons learned from failure. I believe such an environment sends a strong message: we are a company that wants to grow, and we understand that sometimes we're going to fail. But we will deal with failure by understanding, accepting, and figuring out the lessons that we've learned.

7. Make sure you have the basics in place. A quick assessment of the condition of the office, pay scale, and employee morale goes a long way in figuring out whether your business is in a position to start providing intrinsic motivation. It may cost a little more, but it is miniscule compared to the productivity and improved culture that both you and your business will enjoy.

8. Finally, smile. The scientific proof is there; it helps your employees also smile and creates a positive environment in the workplace.

PREDICTING THE UNKNOWNS—*RISK MANAGEMENT & SUSTAINABILITY*

Some risks that are thought to be unknown, are not unknown. With some foresight and critical thought, some risks that at first glance may seem unforeseen, can in fact be foreseen. Armed with the right set of tools, procedures, knowledge and insight, light can be shed on variables that lead to risk, allowing us to manage them.

—*Daniel Wagner,*
Author of Global Risk Agility and Decision Making

We live in volatile times, a statement that's being thrown at us constantly through news outlets. But haven't we always lived in volatile times? What's essentially changed now is the speed by which we see and notice this volatility. This speed simply scares us and leads us to believe that we cannot predict, let alone control, these mysterious "volatile" forces, when in reality we are stronger than we think!

Under these circumstances, SMBs feel the impact more than most. Because of their limited resources, volatility—events like shifts in consumer demands, political climate, or economic cycles, etc.—can deal a nasty blow that could leave them out of business.

SMBs are often frustrated because they are blindsided by events that could have been prevented. There are too many variables to take into consideration, e.g. funding, recessions, competition, internal processes, etc. What weakens the SMBs position is not the volatility but their belief that volatility is abnormal, when in reality, volatility is as natural as the four seasons that we enjoy every year. We pull out our warmer clothes when winter approaches and our lighter ones for summer. Volatility is that natural! It's just dependent on how we view it and prepare for it.

SMBs need to become proficient risk managers. Unfortunately, risk management is a term that puts people off. It's earned a bad reputation as an overcomplicated process that produces things we already know in a more complex form. It is viewed as a superficial process that is a waste of effort, when in truth, it only requires a methodical deliberation on what the problems are.

In this chapter, we will address:

1. Understanding the Landscape
2. Prioritizing the Risks
3. Developing Mitigation Strategies
4. Embedding Sustainability

Understanding the Landscape

Think of a risk landscape as a way to identify all the challenges that your business has to deal with, be they internal or external. The main purpose of the landscape is to be clear about what the fears and challenges are, by writing them down. We will go through a few more steps before we have a complete assessment of these challenges and where to focus your attention.

Throughout this chapter, the terms "risk" and "challenges" are used interchangeably.

Internal Challenges

One way to identify the internal challenges is to sit at your desk with a pen and paper and jot down all the internal challenges that your business is facing. This process, while efficient, provides a skewed view, that is yours alone. Engage with your senior team and deliberate on the key challenges that your business is facing. If you are a management team of 1, then try and bounce this list off your mastermind group.

Recall the Business Self-Assessment analysis that was done at the onset of this book. It should help you get clarity on some of these challenges. The key question is: "Does this challenge/risk impact the business or not?" If it impacts the business, it goes on the list without much detail, simple! Don't overcomplicate it. Include challenges to your operating model, people, financing, etc.

External Challenges

External challenges are different. These include challenges that are external to the business, come in different shapes and sizes, and are sometimes hard to articulate, e.g. economic cycles, industry challenges, impact of competition, disruptors and so on.

It is important to look at all of this in the context of the Destination that you are trying to achieve. Approach it as:

- You know where the business is today.
- You know where you want the business to go.
- You have charted your journey.
- You know what your internal challenges are.
- Now you need to figure out what could potentially throw you off course and prevent the business from reaching its intended Destination.

View these challenges using the following lenses:

1. Industry (including your competition)
2. Economy
3. Reputation
4. Regulations
5. Others

Industry

Industries, as we discussed earlier, go through different life cycles. It's important to know where your industry is at and where it's heading.

Identify what your disruptors are looking like. When you go to trade conferences, when you speak to people or your competitors in social settings, you need to assess where the next disruption is coming from. Your customers are your best source of information on this, because they will give you a sense of what challenges you will face in the future. These can be little hints of information. I would encourage you to not only think of it as what could the next disruptor perspective, but to also consider a potential need and how to address it.

Another very valuable source to identify these risks is your team and your mastermind group. These are all different sources that you can tap to get a better appreciation of the industry risks you're facing. List all the risks and work challenges here.

Economy

Before we discuss the status of the economy and how that impacts you, you need to watch the YouTube video, "How the Economic Machine Works," by Ray Dalio. It's probably one of the best explanations of how the macro economy works; it's only 30 minutes, but very impactful. Summarizing it, the economy goes through two types of cycles: the short-term and the long-term debt cycles, each with a peak and a trough. The short-term debt cycle is of 5–8 years and the long-term one is of 7–9 years. After every boom, there's a recession, and after every recession, there's a boom. It's a cycle that continues, and will continue, until the end of time.

It's not an exact science; that's why it's a range of years. What we have to be aware of is that cycles occur and will always be there. What we cannot predict is the precise timing and the size of these cycles—when the boom starts, when does it end, and how big of a boom or a bust it is.

Understanding these cycles is critical to your business because it can give you an indication of whether your business is in an economic climate that is experiencing a boom or a bust. Your decisions would differ greatly depending on what point the economy is at in the cycle.

Trying to predict when a cycle begins or ends is a guaranteed way to lose money. The best that you can do is prepare for it; be careful in planning and what you are spending money on.

Please note that this is not a lesson in macro-economics. This is an introduction. There's a lot of self-learning that's required, but if you want to start and get on a solid footing quickly, the YouTube video by Ray Dalio is a recommended place to start.

The questions that you need to ask yourself when determining your economy-related external risk are: What stage of the cycle are we on? How susceptible are we to these cycles? Is our industry one that's related to products essential to people's daily lives or to a luxury item?

Other matters to consider are: will you take a loan when the recession is looming? Your immediate reaction may be no. I would say, actually, it depends on what you intend to do with the money. Is the money going to be slotted for expanding your production facility that will take a couple of years to come to fruition? Then, yes, potentially, if you invest in the recession time, you're ready for additional capacity when the boom begins.

Once you acknowledge and accept that this is a cyclical matter, you should not be surprised when a boom ends or a recession begins. Because unfortunately, most SMBs believe that there's always going to be an upward trajectory and that it will never stop. That's incorrect. There is always a recession right after a boom. The more you start monitoring and educating yourself about this, the better you become at understanding the cycles, where you are, and where your business stands within these different cycles.

Stress on how the economic cycle impacts your earnings and cash. There is a critical distinction between them: earnings and cash. This is vital for your survival. Because if your earnings get hit, yet your cash flow is still positive and you're in good shape, that indicates that this is a healthy company and can sustain. However, if you're worried about the earnings but you're neglecting the cash, and your cash is under constraint once the recession hits, you're left in a position where your company could potentially fold.

The key question is, how would a recession or a boom impact my earnings and how would a recession or boom impact my cash?

Reputation
The prevalence of social media has provided every customer a megaphone to reach out to the world. It's a very problematic situation, and managing a reputation is paramount to sustaining a business for the long term. If your reputation gets damaged, how you react to that damage or bad news will reflect on how you're able to sustain, or grow, or stay around for a few years. Some companies have been destroyed by a bad reputation.

Social media giant, Snapchat, had a blow dealt to it when both Kylie Jenner and Rhianna said that they were going to drop Snapchat. Regardless of their reasons, or whether Snapchat was guilty of the accusations, the stock took a tumble. Snapchat is struggling. That was one of my not-so-good investments.

In 2013, a communications specialist was on her way to South Africa. Before she boarded the plane, Justine Sacco posted the following message on her Twitter account, "Going to Africa. Hope I don't get AIDS. Just kidding. I'm white!" What happened next was astonishing. The tweet went viral. By the time Justine got off the plane, she had been fired, there was an angry mob waiting for her at the airport, her entire life had been turned upside down.

The aspects of this occurrence I find most interesting were 1) Justine posted several other tweets earlier that day of a similar nature, but they never caught any traction, and 2) she only had 170 followers. Imagine that impact! So, you can now better understand the potential impact of social media and how that can affect your business.

You need to contemplate your risks from the perspective of the reputation of your business, by assessing your reputation and what can potentially impact it, as well as evaluate how serious the damage from that would be. This needs to be incorporated in your daily decisions, be they about the quality of your products or services or which suppliers to use. These are all related to your business.

I'll give you another example. Lego decided to team up with Shell, since there's a large quantity of petrochemicals that go into the production of Lego. Meanwhile, Greenpeace had been trying to impact Shell because of drilling in the Arctic. Greenpeace released a video depicting an oil drilling operation in the Arctic made from Lego pieces. The scene was set to a sad song in the background before showing oil seeping through and flooding the entire area. The striking visual led to Lego pulling out of the partnership within a week, and the controversy led to Shell temporarily shelving their plans for Arctic drilling.

Be careful who you team up with, who you partner with, who you donate money to because all these factors could impact your reputation. A good litmus test is to ask yourself: If this shows up on social media tomorrow, how would it look? Is that acceptable or is it going to create a significant, or even irreversible, problem?

Regulations

This is a tricky one. In the sense that there's a lot of extra-territorial legislation that is prevalent: the UK anti-bribery act or the US Foreign Corrupt Practices Act. These are all regulations that you have to comply with if you do any business with companies or people from the UK or USA.

The minute you start going cross borders, there's an added complexity, and you have to understand the impact of the various regulations. Not forgetting that you still have to comply with the regulations of where you are based and located. Some companies want to stretch the compliance aspect a bit too far, a point on which to be wary, because it can impact your reputation, it can affect your cash flow or attract criminal charges; and that can be the kiss of death to your business.

Others

The industry, economy, reputation, and regulations are broad categories that help organize your mindset, but they are not the only categories. Identifying risks is a process that is unique to every business; no two businesses have the same risk landscapes.

Consider what aspects are unique to your business and what risk categories require total clarity. List those categories and identify unique challenges to each.

For the sake of emphasis, please reach out to people in your business whom you trust, or the mastermind group, to identify the risks or challenges that you are facing. Diligence in this matter leads to long-term reward.

Prioritizing the Risks

Now that all the risks and challenges have been identified, they need to be prioritized. In this section, we will use a simple tool to help prioritize these risks, to focus efforts on tackling the most critical ones first.

Risks/challenges are rated from three key dimensions:

1. Likelihood: How likely is this event going to happen?
2. Impact: If it happens, how hard will it hit my business, financially and reputationally?
3. Control: How much control do we have over this risk materializing?

You can use the form at the end of the chapter or you can download the Excel sheet www. breakingceilings.com/forms .

Be sure to list all the pertinent risks/challenges regardless of number, so long as you don't go beyond point of productivity; it can get overwhelming and counterproductive. At the end of the day, we want to focus on the key items.

Before we begin the rating, list all the risks in the form or Excel sheet. For each risk, rate it from a likelihood, impact, and control perspective. The following will guide you through the evaluation process.

Likelihood
What to Measure:
When it comes to likelihood, you need to put a percentage on how much you think this is going to happen. Is there a 25% chance? 30% chance? 80% chance?

This is your best estimate, but you need to be honest and not too optimistic with it. I would actually encourage you to be a bit more pessimistic. This needs to reflect your best estimate.

How to Measure

Next to each risk, under the likelihood column on your worksheet, indicate the percentage that best reflects the likelihood/probability of the risk happening.

Impact
What to Measure:

For the sake of simplicity, and without complicating the risk assessment or the prioritization, I want you to look at it strictly from a financial and reputational aspect. More established risk management functions and standards use a more elaborate way to measure risk. The problem is, the minute you start adding more dimensions of impact, it becomes more cumbersome and complicated and probably won't give you much more benefit.

How to Measure

Indicate next to each risk, under the impact column, the financial damage that might occur if this risk materializes. Just give it a dollar amount, but stay consistent in denominations, i.e. $356,000 can be entered as either 356,000 or 356 or .356, and so on.

Control
What to Measure:

For every one of the risks you identified, you or your business may exert a certain level of control. This level of control is on a spectrum from *no control at all* to *fully under control*. It is possible to argue endlessly about how the spectrum should be gauged, so for the sake of simplifying, there are three levels of control:

1. Under control
2. Some control
3. No or limited control

How to Measure

For each one of the risks, put a number from 1 to 3, indicating the level of control you believe you have.

For Under Control, enter 1.
For Some Control, enter 2
For No or limited, control enter 3.

Results

Once you've rated all the risks, you plot them on a bubble chart. You can either download the free Excel sheet from www.breakingceilings.com/forms or build your own worksheet, but keep in mind that:

- Likelihood is on the X-axis
- Control is on the Y-axis
- Impact is the bubble size or Z-axis

Example Risk-Rating Worksheet:

Risk (Short Name)	Risk Description	Likelihood	Impact (in thousands)	Control
Quality	Erosion in the quality of our products	10%	350	1
Financing	Inability to obtain necessary financing for expansion	25%	1,000	2
Competition	Our competition lowers their prices by more than 20%	80%	350	3
Employees Turnover	Key employee(s) leave during next year	20%	150	2
Customer Complaints	Increase in customer complaints by more than 10% from last year	50%	186	3

Revenue decline	Losing 2 or more key clients, resulting in more than 12% of annual budgeted revenue	75%	1,200	2
Recession	Economy has been on a boom for the last 3 years, potential impact of recession	50%	620	1
Regulatory	Possible city regulations on quality control requirements	70%	78	1

How it looks like in Bubble Chart:

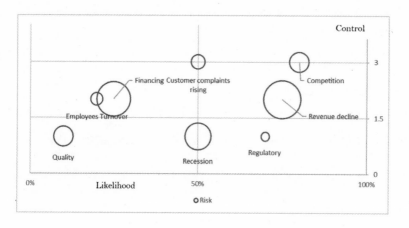

Interpreting the Chart

The chart serves as a tool that helps concentrate your focus on what matters most. When placed into a quadrant perspective, four quadrants emerge. The following diagram will aid in the explanation:

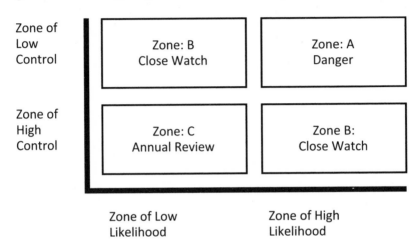

Zone A: Danger

Risks that appear in this zone are those with a high likelihood and low control. They are worth your consistent attention. Now, the size of the bubble will give you a sense of your worst-case scenario. You should do whatever you can to push those bubbles either downwards, i.e. apply more control, or to the left, i.e. reduce likelihood (refer to mitigation strategies on next pages). Risks here require a monthly check-in.

Zone B: Close Watch

Zone B takes up most of the space on the chart, and for good reason. It contains sleeping giants that could be damaging and usually slide under the radar due to the false pretense that it's a low likelihood or "we got this under control" assumption. Best to keep a close eye on these risks. They require a quarterly check-in.

Zone C: Annual Review

Risks here are of low likelihood and strong controls. This is where, ideally, you would want all your risks to be. But that is an impossible task, and if they actually are, then you are not being honest and are missing some serious issues facing your business. Risk here should be reviewed annually.

Explaining the Chart by Zones:

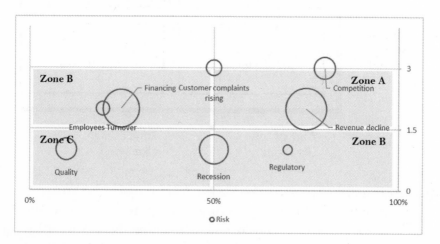

Bubbles that Cross into More than One Zone

If you notice, the recession risk is right on the cusp of 50% likelihood and is spread along 2 zones, B and C. This is natural and will occur regularly; in these instances, err on the side of the higher risk zone. In this case, consider it as Zone B.

Final Words of Caution

Risk management is a subjective process; it is only as good as your understanding of the situation and the data that you use. Apply scrutiny, sound judgement, and consult.

Remember, it is a tool, and to get the best readings, you need to use multiple tools to completely understand where things are presently.

Developing Mitigation Strategies

In reality, there are only 4 mitigation strategies that could be used.

Accept

Sometimes you just have to accept the risk and move on with it. There is not much that can be done here except keeping an eye on how matters are developing and taking it day by day.

Transfer

This mitigation strategy includes two options: 1) get it insured or 2) get someone else to do it for you. As for the insurance option, I would encourage you to seek specialized advice in this field. A good advisor can save you a lot of money over time and provide you with options that you may be unaware existed.

Limit

The simple explanation of the limit strategy is applying controls to reduce either the likelihood or impact of the risk. This is done by changing a process, building a wall, or taking some form of action.

Avoid

Simply walk away and don't approach it. This is probably one of the hardest things to do and requires a considerable level of discipline. There are cases in life where fighting that battle is just not worth it.

Embedding Sustainability

Finally, think of risk management as a tool for your sustainability. And by sustainability, I don't mean the green sustainability, but the sustainability of your business into the future. Identifying and understanding the challenges you're facing is the first step, and it will help you to better prepare yourself for these risks.

It is essential to keep in mind that it's not an exact science. Risk management is a combination of science and art. It improves by having external and internal conversations, data gathering and analysis, educating yourself about what's happening around you. It's critical that you are clear about the challenges you're facing and the various data inputs that you receive.

Remember, do the assessment 2 or 3 times a year. It has the potential to save your business!

Afterthought

It is tempting to dismiss risk management; if you are a business owner who has relied on their wits and tenacity to make it, you would say, "It's all in here," while pointing to either your head or your heart. That may be true, but to grow your business and break those ceilings that are preventing you from getting to where you want to be, you need to have decision systems, and risk management is an important part of decision systems. The "here" will only get you so far; be smart and try to predict the unknowns; I guarantee you somebody else is already doing it!

NAVIGATION

What's measured improves.

—Peter Drucker

If you were to observe the flight path of an aircraft going from Singapore to JFK, you will never find it to be a straight line. The pilots have to continuously check the instruments and adjust course throughout the flight, following a predetermined path. The note here is that the path is never a straight line, and instruments and dials are needed to keep them on course.

Similarly, a business must apply the same rigor of the pilots, constantly checking the dials and adjusting course, on a predetermined path to reach the destination of choice. Some days, you will have good weather and tail winds, and on other days, you will have to fly through storms and headwinds. Regardless, you keep pushing through and reading the dials to help you navigate to your destination.

In this section, we're going to review the different navigation tools that are required to stay on your predetermined path. As we now know, what gets measured gets done!

UNLOCKING CASH FLOW
SECRETS—*MONEY*

*Business is an intellectual sport; anyone who plays this game with
their emotions, gut, and glands get killed. There is simply not a way
to get lucky sustainably. GUT is an acronym for (Gave Up Thinking).*

— *Keith J. Cunningham*

<u>INTRODUCTION</u>

Imagine this scenario: it is that time of the month; the financial reports
are ready, and you have blocked time in your calendar to review them. You
go first to the income statement, and your eyes inadvertently look at the
bottom line, the coveted net profit. Is it above budget? Yes. Are sales up?
Yes, all looks good! So why then are we struggling with our cash position?
Your meeting with the bank later in the day is looming over you like a dark
cloud.

Unfortunately, this is a common problem, mainly with SMBs. Why? Good
question, because somehow the business gets all wrapped up in the growth
trap and forgets one of the oldest and most important tenets, *"It's not what
you make, it's what you keep."* Let that sink in for a minute. Having an 80%
net income margin is worthless if you are paying most of it to offset loans

or if most of the receivables are over 180 days due. Net income is one of the most misleading figures in any financial statement. It is a number that can be manipulated easily through creative accounting practices, like simply changing the expected life of assets: a completely non-cash impacting transaction that makes your net income look good.

Cash is the blood that runs in the veins of your business, delivering much needed oxygen to the different parts operating, to keep the business going. By sheer will to exist, cash should be fiercely guarded and protected against waste, as every drop of it counts. Practically every decision the business makes has an impact on cash. With that said, we can surmise that the basic premise of any business is to convert its assets into revenue, and revenues into profits, and profits into cash, simple.

Let us try that with a couple of examples:

1. You need a new laptop, so like most of us, you go for the higher processing power, bigger storage, and larger memory, to handle all your needs. It costs you $3,000. Applying the process, how will that $3,000 translate into cash back into your pocket? Will the higher capacity laptop do the job better than the $900 one? The answer is no, it will not, unless you are in the graphic design business where you need specialized equipment. In that case, yes, a larger capacity laptop could help you deliver better quality work and more cash back to you. Now apply that to larger assets: a car, a new office space, etc. Always tie it back to the formula: assets, revenue, profit, and cash.

2. Acquiring another company. Slightly more complicated than buying a laptop, nevertheless, by applying the same principles we would need to understand how the business we are acquiring converts its assets into revenues, into profits, into cash. If they are doing a lousy job at it, then we walk away. If they are being effective, efficient, and productive, then the deal is worth looking into.

There are numerous considerations that are not the objective of this book. The idea is, the formula works.

In a way, that is what this chapter is all about. It aims at setting a framework to measure the performance of your business and at how you can start looking at what really matters; after all, it's all about what you keep.

BASICS

During my years in the consulting world, I often looked with bewilderment at CEOs who, when pressured, gathered the executive team, expressed their discontent with the results, and barked orders at them to "fix it." That CEO then walked away, expecting that his team would see how bad he felt and out of sheer fear go about and fix the problem of staggering sales. Imagine if the roles were reversed, and that angry CEO was at the receiving end; how many similar stressful meetings would it take to disengage her from the business or push her to walk away? I bring this up because it is truly astonishing that some leaders still think that this is a method of getting better results.

To change the results of a business, decisions need to be made; decisions are transformed into activities, and activities change results. There is no other way. The correlation is clear and has always been clear. If you wish to change the results of a business, then you need to change activities within the business!

Before diving into the different measurement tools, it is important to clear out a few basic principles. These are needed for you to be able to understand where the business is going and how to steer in the direction of choice.

Reading Numbers

Business is a language of numbers. The numbers tell stories of what is going on with the business, where it is weak, where it is strong, where value is hiding, and where it is eroding. The ability to read these numbers and decipher them does not come intuitively to most of us. Instead, it requires effort, discipline, and time. I was at a conference once, and the speaker claimed that it took Warren Buffet 9 years to be able to understand the business language of numbers. Whether right or wrong isn't the point; it simply serves to emphasize the importance of reading the numbers and the effort required to do so. I beg you not to be one of the business owners who looks at the income statement, glances at the balance sheet, and quickly skips to the cash flow statement. That is, if it is actually prepared in the first place. Each one of these statements tells you part of the story. Learn them well; there are numerous online courses, books, and blogs that would help. I would recommend you start with a personal favorite of mine, a book by Keith J. Cunningham, *The Ultimate Blueprint for an Insanely Successful Business*: short, straight, to the point, full of insights, and quite impactful.

Good Records

Your business must, with no exceptions, maintain clear, organized, sufficiently detailed, and complete records. Be it in Excel, or any other system, having good records is fundamental to monitoring your business and taking the best decisions possible. A good measure is to ask your accounts team to give you the sales trend of the last 2 years. If it takes more than 60 minutes to get it, there is something wrong. This is considered basic functionality. Trouble follows if you don't get an income statement, balance sheet, and cash flow statement as part of your month-end report.

This is an area where you need a little investment to have a decent accounting system that meets your needs. Several are online and fairly cheap. The business does not need to spend thousands of dollars to have basic functionality; those days are a thing of the past.

Basis of Accounting

It is unfortunate, but some businesses still maintain their records on the cash basis of accounting. While it may work for early stages and for a little while, you need to have accrual basis of accounting. No two ways around that; if you want your business to grow, you need to be able to read where your business is going, and that can only be provided by accrual basis. Do not allow your accountant to defend the cash basis; this is not useful to your business.

Books of Account

When it comes to books of account:

1. Don't mix your personal records with that of the company. If you are charging certain personal expenses to the business, log them in separate books. The business reports should be free from any of these types of alien charges to the business.

2. The tax laws differ depending on the country or jurisdiction you are in. In some countries, tax laws are based on cash basis, e.g. USA, and in others, it is accrual basis, e.g. Canada. If you are in a cash basis tax system, then you will need to maintain two sets of accounts, one for financial accounting (accrual basis) and the other for taxes (cash basis). This is not tax evasion or fraud; this is to provide accurate reports. Having books of accounts on cash basis may be acceptable to the tax authorities but is disastrous to your business.

3. Hire a good accountant to handle this. Capable accountants will organize your accounts in a way that will allow for easy extraction of detailed reports.

Cash Test

When making decisions related to the business, always keep in mind the Cash Test, which basically assesses whether the decision you are about to take will either:

1. *Effectively* convert assets into revenues?
2. *Efficiently* convert revenues into profits?
3. *Productively* convert profits into cash?

In other words, what you should be looking at is the impact of that decision on the business's operating cash flow. Here is how it looks in a formula:

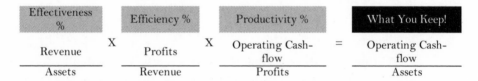

A business where operating cash flow is higher than assets is a healthy business. It becomes healthier the more the multiples are; so, a business where operating cash flow is four times the assets is performing much better than one where the cash flow is twice the assets.

BUSINESS DASHBOARD

These are the dials that should be on your business dashboard.

Cash Flow

Oddly, there are three groups of cash flow: operating, financing, and investing. Any cash flow statement would include these three groups. If this is the statement that you gloss over when you look at the monthly reports your accounting team prepares, well...knock it off! This is the most important statement. Learn it well and understand all the secrets it tells you.

- **Operating Cash Flow:**
  Represents all the cash that was collected and paid out through the normal course of business, like receiving revenue and paying bills.

  The bulk of transactions that run through your business will show up here, so keep a close eye on it. This is probably the most meaningful dial because a successful business should return cash to its shareholders in proportion to the assets that have been deployed.

  Negative operating cash flow indicates that the business is unable to sustain itself from its own operations, usually triggering the need to borrow money or inject more capital.

- **Financing Cash Flow:**
  Shows all the cash that has been received from bank loans and facilities, as well as all the loan repayments that were made.

  Tip: whenever operating cash flow is negative, you will usually see an increase in the financing cash flow.

- **Investing Cash Flow:**
  Every time your business invests in assets or receives cash returns from the sale of these assets, it will show under this heading.

Receivables and Payables

The key when dealing with receivables and payables is understanding the different payment terms for each and their respective impact on your business. For example, if your business offers customers payment terms of 30 days and pays its vendors within 15 days, this mismatch means that cash will exit the business a lot faster than it was received. This strains your cash flow and eventually, if not addressed, would lead the business to seek funds from other sources, like borrowing or capital injection. As the leader, you should always keep an eye on the balance between payment and credit terms.

Here are some ideas of what you can do to restore the balance:

1. Identify what the right balance is:
   The Accounting/Finance team needs to figure out what the right balance is for the business. It is not as straightforward as both having to be equal. There are many considerations like volume, industry norms, turnover, long-term commitments, etc. This analysis requires skill; if your business doesn't have that skill in-house, there is no harm in acquiring external assistance.
2. Renegotiate with vendors and customers:
   If there are long-term contracts in place, it would be more challenging but not impossible to change them. Come up with a different value proposition, maybe offer more services, or shorter lead time, etc. Nothing is impossible, just requires resourcefulness!
3. Reach out to your sales and procurement teams and incentivize them to maintain this balance or, better yet, improve it.

Inventory

Typically, a business adds value to customers by providing them with products, services, or both. In either case, there is some sort of inventory sitting somewhere. If it's a product-based company, as in physical product, that product is being assembled or manufactured. If it's a service, there is some sort of capacity sitting somewhere, e.g. people, server space, etc. To keep the cash flow positive, the inventory needs to be moving as fast as possible. The more it moves out to the clients, the better the impact on cash flow, provided that pricing and collection are also handled well.

This definition of inventory is slightly different from the traditional accounting sense of it, as it considers the capacity being built within the business to serve its customers. The question is how to monitor it so that cash is not tied up for longer periods of time. It is rather difficult to provide one formula that fits all types of businesses; one rule does *not* fit all!

The key is to link the inventory to the sales and collection process. Questions like:

1. What is the average time it takes the business to collect one dollar from the time the raw material is procured till the time the receivable is collected?
2. If this average time is reduced, will it save on cash flow requirements? If yes, by how much, and if no, why not?
3. What changes are needed in the business to reduce that time? Consider impact on operations, logistics, sales team, accounting, etc.

Revenue and Cost Analysis (RCA)

All business owners, one may hope, review the Profit & Loss statement (P&L) regularly and consistently. Nevertheless, is a P&L really telling you what is going on in a business and how your cash is impacted? I would argue that the summary P&L that sits on the top of most management reports does not do that. It only shows the results of the operations for a set period of time, and that's fine. A summary P&L serves a different audience. The leader needs to get into a more detailed understanding of this critical dial.

The power of the Revenue and Cost Analysis (RCA) comes from building relations, and not necessarily from the end result that the P&L shows. These questions would help clarify the point:

1. How were our revenues, costs, and profits impacted by the latest marketing campaign?
2. Did the changes to the production process reduce cost or not?
3. Has the business grown since the previous year?

The RCA evaluates how the business is behaving by comparing the results from one point in time to another. There are multiple ways to carry out this analysis. Each leader has personal preferences on to execute this, so here are some basic ideas or principles to help:

1. *What's the Decision?*
    It cannot be stressed enough, the information that you need depends on the decision that you are trying to make. As odd as that may sound, it is true. For example, if a business is considering closing down one of its three locations to cut costs, one would suppose that the choice would be as easy as closing down the location that has the lowest net profit. However, this isn't the case, as there are other dimensions; the one with the least profit could be the distribution hub for the other three. Closing it down would result in a logistical nightmare. Similar mistakes have been made repeatedly by businesses, so be careful.

2. *Compare multiple years*
    It's all about relationships or trends, so having a few prior year numbers will go a long way. Consider having the current year in months and 4 prior years. Then you can study the trend and better understand how your business has been behaving.

3. *Devil in the Details*
    Not all analyses are created equal, so make sure that there is sufficient detail in the line items you are analyzing, to give reasonable results. Meaning, if you just analyze cost of sales as one-line item you will not get the real benefit. Instead, go down to all the cost elements of your product or service.

4. *Use Different Lenses*
    Looking at trends and comparing years is a powerful analytical tool. To make it even more powerful, consider the relationship within the same year by comparing costs to the revenue. As in, what is the percentage of packaging cost to revenue?

Usually the analyses are performed on the total line item, but have you considered doing an RCA for one/unit product or service? For example, what are the cost components of a single box of tissues or an hour of labor? It definitely changes your perspective when you look at it that way.

Budgets

Just the mere mention of the word "budget" makes the majority of people cringe, including myself. Budgets have become the bane of existence for certain people. I have always questioned why budgets have this effect on people. Wouldn't you want a reference point to measure against? A yardstick to tell you how successful you are at achieving the predetermined goal? Something to keep you on track? Well, yes, every business should have them, but what happened was that business heads started using them in the most destructive ways.

Anywhere from July to November every year, businesses start preparing budgets for the following year. You can almost feel the stress in the air when that process begins: meetings, analyses, heated debates, stretched targets, quantum physics, and so on. The business leader then takes the budget and goes through the first fierce round of negotiations to reduce costs and increase sales targets, to the chagrin of many employees. Then he takes it to the decision-makers, and another round of negotiations and threats ensues. Always the same cycle and always an annual budget.

Dear leaders, a budget is a tool by which a business predicts how it will perform in the coming period. These predictions are based on assumptions. So, we penalize employees for not achieving their budget targets based on predictions and assumptions. Where is the logic in that? So much emphasis is placed on budgets, and the real questions are left unanswered.

To begin with, a budget should be part of a Journey Map. It demonstrates where the business wants to go and identifies the resources and requirements needed to grow to the next level, and it should span upwards of one year; 3–5 would be ideal. Most, if not all, sustainable growth initiatives need time to materialize and return the anticipated benefits.

This does not mean that a budget should be set and left for 3 years; that is a recipe for disaster. Instead, have annual meetings to update the budget, analyze what went right and what went wrong, revisit the assumptions and improve them, and revise the targets and the time frame. My plea to you, dear leaders, is use it as a tool and do not turn it into a terrorizing experience. Let your team flourish and grow.

Governance

Whenever the word "governance" pops up in a conversation, you will notice some people openly cringe or roll their eyes; the conversation usually goes in a different direction after that. The unfortunate common belief is that once you start discussing governance, then there is a whole set of complicated procedures, charters, and lack of flexibility that makes achieving your goal more tiresome. Needless to argue, there is partial merit to that common belief, but what if we saw governance through an altered lens? What would you say to this claim: governance has a direct and strong impact on your cash flow! Wouldn't you change your mind about governance? Don't believe it? Let us explore that claim.

As the leader, sitting in your office, keeping a close eye on the instruments (reports) at your disposal, have you ever taken into account the cost of having all these instruments (reports)? How many people are involved in putting a report together? How many layers of approval are needed before a decision is made? How reliable are the reports to determine where the business is going?

These are all good questions, but how are they impacting cash flow? Here is how:

1. Organization Structure
2. Process Efficiency
3. Mastermind Effectiveness

Organization Structure

Did you ever consider how well the organization structure and decision-making process support the value your business delivers to your customers?

If you are delivering a product or service that has low cost as one of its value offerings, then having a multi-layered organization with centralized decision-making is bleeding your cash. You see, information in multi-layered organizations travels slower and doesn't always reach the decision-makers undiluted. Remember the game "telephone" you played as a child? A line of several children, where one repeats words in the ear of the child next to him as they were heard and so on, until the last one reveals the words, which usually turn out to be gibberish. That is exactly what happens to your reports. And along every layer, someone is spending time and company resources to add a little to the report and pass it upwards.

In contrast, if your value drivers consist of offering the latest cutting-edge products to your customers, then your organization structure needs to reflect and support an aggressive R&D function and a prompt decision-making process.

Key Learning: Complex organization structures and centralized decision-making cost money in the form of added cost and lost opportunities. Simplify and empower!

Process Efficiency

Often, I see companies hire a consulting firm to create their *policies and procedures* for them. It has become such a commodities service offering with the consulting firms that many reputable firms have actually stopped the practice. Unfortunately, consultants end up creating these elaborate *policies and procedures* manuals that get shelved rather quickly. This is because they impose impractical layers of authority. I worked with a client several years ago where a payment had literally 6 signatures on it before it was issued.

Building layers and layers of controls is useless and drains you of cash because your resources, employees and systems, are burdened with unnecessary steps and prevent people from carrying out mission-critical tasks. Worse off, you have to hire more people to comply with controls.

I am not saying that you don't need structure and process. On the contrary, I am saying you need to have well-designed controls, efficient and effective, and not always rely on consultants to do that for you. A couple of good measures:

1.   How long is your *policy and procedure* manual? If it is more than 20 pages, you have a problem.
2.   Can you put the process on one A4 size flowchart with legible font? If not, you have a problem.

Key Learning: Simplify your processes, and don't overburden the business with excessive control. Simplify and empower!

Mastermind Effectiveness

A mastermind is: "Coordination of knowledge and effort, in a spirit of harmony, between 2 or more people, for the attainment of a definite purpose" (Napoleon Hill, *Think and Grow Rich*). Does that sound familiar? Well, it should be the definition of the Board of Directors, or at least that is what it was intended to be. Unfortunately, boards are rarely a group of knowledgeable people working in a spirit of harmony to attain a definite goal. They have become status symbols, rife with politics and members who have limited awareness of the company's business.

The boards are usually dominated by either the CEO or the Chairman of the Board. The danger with that dominance and the board's ineffectiveness means that the decisions being made are the brainchild of a single individual, regardless of who it is. One person cannot be right all the time; that is why we need the collective efforts of a group of individuals.

Various companies throughout history have failed because of a failure in governance at the board level. Examples: Enron had world-class board governance, on paper that is. British Petroleum faced governance failure where the board did not take the lead position in dealing with a crisis at that level. But these are all mega corporations, so how are they comparable to you?

Most small and medium ships don't have boards; they have friends whom the leader calls upon from time to time. So, ask yourself this: who do you go to when you need advice? Is it the same person every time, a long-time friend or mentor? You do get value from that person. Now, imagine if you had carefully thought through the diverse types of advice that you require and put together a group of people that could provide that advice, get them to meet regularly, and discuss how you can attain your destination. How powerful would that be? How focused would your business become?

Some advice on how to form the mastermind group:

- Instead of calling it a board of directors and attaching a stigma to it, call it a board of advisors or simply the mastermind.
- Choose the individuals carefully and make sure there is harmony amongst them. Everyone needs to be on the same page when it comes to attaining the destination.
- You need to compensate them; no one will give you that time and dedication for free. Compensation does not have to be money; it can be services in kind or any other sort of compensation that you could muster up.
- Meet frequently; with today's technologies this is easier than ever.

But how does that affect cash flow? Think of a board that has members who aren't educated on the business or are disengaged; they would vote on anything put in front of them—problem-laced mergers, unnecessary acquisitions, appointment of unqualified senior management, unrealistic strategies, etc. All these misguided decisions directly cost money and indirectly erode your employee morale, where waste carelessness causes your business to fester.

Cluttered Dashboards
Excessive Key Performance Indicators

"Eighty-seven pages of Key Performance Indicators (KPI) and initiatives!" I exclaimed with shock. "Yes, of course!" replied my client. "How else will one manage the business? This report tells me exactly where every cent is spent and what is going on in my business."

To this day, I cannot believe that any company could have that many KPIs to run their business. Ironically, the business wasn't performing, and that is why I was there. They had run into cash flow issues and needed immediate support.

That example is extreme, but don't underestimate how much time and effort is spent on assembling these KPIs and building reports. It deducts from valuable time, when they should be focusing on managing the business and using a handful of critical KPIs. What is worse, in those 87 pages, not a single KPI was related to operating cash flow, so it was no wonder they ran into trouble.

Be wary of excessive metrics; they detract you from the critical dials we talked about. Focus is key in achieving your goal.

Informal Networks

Another clutter-inducing dial is an invisible yet powerful one - the informal networks within the business, more commonly known as the rumor mill. As the leader, you are torn between using this dial and, simultaneously, dealing with the mess that accompanies it. It can get louder and louder the more attention you pay it. It is tricky to shape or define, difficult to ascertain whether it is truthful or deceitful. The primary way I recommend verifying is to test the information with facts. Presume a whisperer is giving you some selective information—do not react immediately. Try to ascertain the validity of the information with reliable facts. With time, the reliable networks will emerge.

A final word of caution: if you let the informal networks be your sole source of information, you will have a tough time attracting people of value, and in turn, the business will have a hard time creating value.

Need to Know More:

- Book: *The Ultimate Blueprint for an Insanely Successful Business* by Keith J. Cunningham

POWERFUL CORPORATE MINDSET—*LEADERSHIP*

Your mindset matters. It affects everything—from the business and investment decisions you make, to the way you raise your children, to your stress levels and overall well-being.

—*Peter Diamandis*

As a business head, the captain of your ship, you know that rallying your team to a single objective is the difference between prosperity and bankruptcy. It is no easy task; it is one that requires a lot of coaching, parading, tough love, and all else that you can muster. At the core of it, you will require every ounce of energy to make sure your ship, your business, is on track to arrive at its Destination. This task is not for the faint of heart, because the emotional drain on the leader is immense and can quickly manifest into various illnesses of the body, mind, and soul.

To truly be able to influence the organization, you will need to look inwards first, to your own mindset, your own resilience. As the leader, your mindset will affect everyone and everything in your company. In their Harvard Business Review article titled "Social Intelligence and the Biology of Leadership," authors Daniel Goleman and Richard Boyatzis state this interesting fact: "Your behavior can energize—or deflate—your entire organization through mood contagion. For example, if you laugh often and set an easygoing tone, you'll trigger similar behaviors amongst your team members. Shared behaviors unify a team, and bonded groups perform better than fragmented ones."

Several years ago, I was promoted to Partner and given charge of a territory and team. My responsibilities included nearly everything to make the team and territory profitable. Consider it as a CEO for a certain geography. I had a solid strategy, communicated with the team, made sure everyone was aligned, held training sessions—the works. At the end of the year, we made our budget, just barely. That was frustrating because I had thrown everything I had into this and ensured the team was continuously motivated. It would be a couple of years later that I realized why we didn't make the numbers. Simply, it was the result of my mental resilience. I would put on a show of confidence and support every morning, and by the end of the day, I would be drained. I was afraid and confused on what to do. A first-time CEO with limited training on how to manage a large team, and it showed! The team knew it and played along. My fears and confusion transferred to them, and they behaved according to that.

I have come a long way since then and have learned a valuable truth. The team will read me irrespective of how brave a show I put on, so it's better to be authentic and strong. So, if you constantly feel tired, bogged down, and don't have time to think, then realize that your company is feeling the same. To change that, begin with changing yourself.

This chapter is about just that; to fix, galvanize, or change your corporate mindset, you must and need to start with taking care of your mindset—the leader's mindset.

The Leader's Mindset

Humans are, after all, creatures of habit. Will Durant said it so perceptively, "We are what we repeatedly do. Excellence, then, is not an act, but a habit." A quote often attributed to Aristotle. What it refers to is that obtaining and keeping a resilient mindset is a matter of habit, and creating new habits requires a great deal of self-discipline. A resilient mindset is the result of nourishing three key elements:

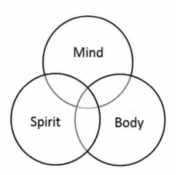

Why these three? These elements reflect our nature as humans—we are tri-beings as we consist of *mind, body, and spirit.* Looking at ourselves from these three elements allows us to better understand our needs, reactions, behaviors, ups and downs, more deeply. All three are linked and inter-twined with each other; if one hurts, the other two will feel it and react to it; sadly, the reverse is not true. If you take care of one and neglect the others, you will quickly feel the pain and discomfort in the other two ele-ments. It is a bizarre relationship; harming one will harm all, caring for one will not care for all. Continuous nourishment of all three together is necessary, albeit a specific kind of nourishment for each.

Assessment
Before going any further, how about establishing a health-check baseline? There is a questionnaire at the end of this chapter, or you can download it from www.breakingceilings.com/forms. It takes no more than 5 minutes but will at least give you an idea of where you are on healthy habits.

Go ahead! It's truly worth it.

What your score means

If your score is:

- Higher than 55—you have excellent habits that nourish your body, mind, and spirit and keep you focused on achieving your goals.
- Between 30 and 54—your habits are a good starting point, and you could use some help in improving them and the state of your body, mind, and spirit.
- Below 30—there is much you need to reconsider about how you are living your life.

Please remember these are not exact science techniques but give you an indication of where you are and should be treated so. Personal resilience is a journey, and no matter how strong you think you are, life will always test you. So, you have to keep training yourself.

Rituals for the Health of the MIND

The mind is the central orchestrator of thoughts, emotions, and actions. It has the ability to create and destroy, all through thought. This may seem like a bold statement, but it's actually an understatement. The mind is capable of amazing achievements, and we are barely scratching the surface to comprehend its true potential. One very interesting truth is whatever you feed the mind will resonate across all three elements. Meaning, feed it useful, powerful, and inspirational material, then you become useful, powerful, and inspired. Feed it garbage, and you will feel like garbage. So, if you are addicted to amusing YouTube videos and reading romance novels, your mind will manifest those into your daily life.

The general health of your mind is the cornerstone of your overall health and resilience. If you are constantly anxious and worrying about what is going on with this or that, you are bringing yourself and those around you down; it serves no one and especially not you.

Healthy Habits

The path to a healthy and resilient mind can be attributed to three basic steps:

Understand Yourself

Do you know what your triggers are? Why they are the way they are? Why are you so motivated to succeed? These are serious questions that will guide you in your darkest of days and must be answered truthfully. Because if we are to grow, we need to know what forces drive us, how we think and analyze information. Sure, you have been doing well so far. After all, you have a business that has been succeeding.

The obvious question here is, do you know why you want to achieve whatever goal you want? This is probably the most important question you will be challenged with: *Why?* When answered correctly, it will reveal to you the real fear or love that motivates you, and that knowledge is potent. It is easy to say I want to become rich because I don't want to go hungry or avoid negative feelings, but persist and dig deep to understand that honest emotion that drives you.

Figuring out the *why* does not come naturally to us, especially when we ask it directly. Turns out we need to ask ourselves 7 times to get it. Why 7 times? What matters is that you need to do this exercise.

Exercise

Turn off your phone(s) and sit in a quiet, comfortable place. All you have to do is answer 7 simple questions with the utmost of honesty.

Q1. Why is it important to succeed in leading/owning the business you are in?

Q2. Why is it important to [insert the answer from the previous question]?

Q3. Why is it important to [insert the answer from the previous question]?

Q4. Why is it important to [insert the answer from the previous question]?

Q5. Why is it important to [insert the answer from the previous question]?

Q6. Why is it important to [insert the answer from the previous question]?

Q7. Why is it important to [insert the answer from the previous question]?

Shedding a few tears once you answer the seventh question is a common phenomenon and is one of great transformation and empowerment. It is only once you understand what drives you that you can find the inner peace and clarity that will ignite you for the rest of your life. Appreciate that and understand it well.

Here are some more questions that you might want to consider:

1. When is your creative energy at its highest? Morning, noon, or night? Schedule mundane tasks to off-energy times. Make sure you focus on key tasks when you are at your highest energy.

2. How do you solve problems? Being alone? Discussion? Whiteboard or paper pad?
    This will help in solving problems faster. Just surround yourself with your preferred method.

3. What activities give you energy? Exercise, meditation, charity work, reading, walking, etc. Do a lot more of them.

4. What foods make you feel lethargic? Avoid them at times of intense tasks!

5. What food make you feel energized and light? Consume more of them.

Setup

Set yourself up for success, every day!

We all tire from hearing the phrases, "Run the day or it will run you" or "Carpe Diem, Seize the Day." Clichés like these exist for the reason that they are *true*. You must own your morning to own your day. There are no shortcuts, ifs, or buts. Waking up at 11:00 a.m. and expecting to rule the day will just not make it happen. I can never forget my grandmother trying to get me out of bed during our summers with her. "Wake up before the day's blessings are distributed or you don't get any." Simple message that I only grasped later in my life.

Setting up, priming, preparing, or whatever you want to call it, gets you in the right frame of mind for success. All you need is a distinct set of rituals to follow every morning. This may seem like too much to ask, but there is nothing more important that starting your day on the right foot.

Having children who need care in the morning does not simplify this. You need to carve the time out of somewhere else. Waking up 30 minutes earlier would definitely help. Personally, I realized that my morning Setup was so important that I started waking up at 5:30 a.m. to make sure I had enough time to complete my rituals.

These rituals differ from one successful person to another, but they all revolve around the same things: exercise, meditate, read, personal goal, lessons learned, and breakfast. You need to find your own rituals and the sequence that works for you. Here are some examples to help get you started. Remember, take it easy to start with and adjust if it does not work for you:

My Morning Ritual:

1. 5:30 a.m.—Wake up and drink lots of water, then brush teeth.
2. 5:40–6:00 a.m.—Read, mostly books or magazine articles (not the news).

3. 6:00–6:30/40 a.m.—Work out
4. 6:40–7:00 a.m.—Shower
5. 7:00–7:20 a.m.—Meditate
6. 7:20–7:30 a.m.—Recite my goals, personal mantra, and focus on the task of the day
7. 7:30–7:50 a.m.—Breakfast with family
8. 8:00 a.m.—Head out

Other examples:

A brisk walk or run → meditation → write down goals → shower → breakfast.
Meditation → exercise of choice → review goals → breakfast → shower.
Read → meditate → exercise → review goals → breakfast.

Try out what you think will work for you and change as required. There are no hard and fast rules as long as you get your heart pumping, your energy peaked, and your mind focused on the goal of the day.

Condition
Conditioning your mind is the final step and can be achieved by:

1. **Your Words**
   Choose the words you use very carefully; they will manifest into reality. There was a time in my life when I would frequently utter the words 'I am tired." I am tired of this or that, or I can't get enough sleep! Guess what? I was always tired, and everyone around me was tired of me being tired. Once I had become truly fed up with being tired, I decided to change those words into "I am feeling great!" So, whenever I was asked how I was, there was only one answer, "feeling great!" And as expected, I started feeling great, and to some degree, people started feeling great around me.

2. Your Body Language

In one of TED.com's most watched talks, Amy Cuddy's talk titled, "Why your body language may shape who you are," she reveals that we can change other people's perceptions—and perhaps even our own body chemistry—simply by shifting body positions. If you stand up straight and walk proud, people will see that and treat you just as such. Please take time to watch it, it's life-changing.

3. Your Focus

You, and only you, can elect what to focus on. So, if you choose to focus on the lousy day you are having, or on the upcoming stressful board meeting, then that is what your mind will continue to focus on and divert your energy towards. Alternatively, you can choose to focus on learning from experiences that you go through. Elect to grow and apply a growth mindset and not one that is fixed and stagnant, just because that's what you know.

4. Thinking Time

Now, of course, as a business leader you have difficult questions to answer, and you need to focus on these in a particular way. Worrying and steaming over them all day is counterproductive to you. You need to schedule thinking time. This is a great habit to adopt; simply set aside quiet, uninterrupted time, without any devices, to deliberate on problem areas in your business or personal life. Just you, a notepad and pen, sitting or standing in a quiet place. Be ready with your questions and think about how you want to address them. That's it.

5. Goal Setting

One of the single most impactful things to do is to set goals. Every year, you should be clear about the goals that you want to achieve—big or small, business or personal. Place time limits for yourself and go for it. However, to truly benefit from the power of setting goals you must review them on a regular basis. This is where you need self-discipline. Review your goals every 2 months, without fail.

6. **Reading**

   Absolutely essential to growth. You cannot expand your mind without reading for a minimum of 30 minutes each day. Leveraging the various media options of today, you can read, listen to podcasts, watch videos, whatever works for you. Just learn a little every day. There are no shortcuts to this!

7. **Sleeping**

   Do not underestimate the long-term negative impact of sleeping 5–6 hours a night on your body and psyche. You are driven! You have a lot on your plate, and sleep is the first thing that suffers; it doesn't change the science. Hating sleep is a good thing; it means you want to do something with your life.

Just remember, it's not just about quantity but also quality of sleep. Consider taking a sleep test to find out what actually occurs with your body while you sleep. For example, I didn't realize that my brain used to wake up 6–8 times per night and that I seldom went into deep sleep. Through breathing exercises and meditation, I managed to improve my quality of sleep.

As for quantity, it is a tough one to figure out. You will need to experiment to figure out what works for you. The science says minimum of 8 hours/night, but we all know that is difficult to maintain if you are leading an organization. My personal habit is 3 nights of 6-hour sleep, then one good 8-hour sleep and 90-minute naps on the weekend.

Rituals for the Health of the BODY

Your physical health habits are mainly related to exercise and food. This section will not preach to you about what your ideal weight should be or that you need to exercise 3 or 5 times a week. There are many experts in this field, and each one seems to have a slightly contradicting opinion of the other.

You need to understand the impact of food and exercise on your energy levels. The simple rule is, if it increases your energy, then it's a good thing; if it makes you feel lethargic or reduces your energy, avoid it like the plague.

To illustrate this point, start noticing how the food you eat makes you feel afterwards. Ideally, you can keep a journal of what you consume and how it makes you feel; an example is provided at the end of this chapter. This also applies for exercise. Yes, it makes you feel good afterwards, most of the time. Not all exercises impact your body the same. Some forms of exercise are intense and could drain you completely; some people thrive on that, others don't. You only need to listen to your body and what it tells you. I, personally, am energized after a brisk walk. It clears my mind and I feel much improved afterwards, but I still need my weekly intense sweat-producing workouts.

The next section presents some pointers on what you can practice.

Exercise Habits

Running your own business is a daunting task that can consume your 24 hours easily, so finding the time to exercise is always difficult. Exercise works to expel toxins from your body and pumps you with endorphins, but time is scarce. So how do you manage it? Do what a business leader does best—schedule it! Put it on the calendar and mark it with "Do Not Change." If it doesn't get scheduled it won't get done.

After you've scheduled it, let's address the ideal length and frequency of the workouts. The common consensus is 3 times a week, coupled with monitoring your food consumption (quality and quantity). Factoring travel and prep time prior to and post each workout, we can extrapolate anywhere from 1.5 to 2.5 hours, 3 times a week. That's a total of 5–8 hours a week. Would you believe me if I told you that all you needed was one hour a week? Of course not! Fortunately, the advancement of science has generated a new 7-minute workout that incorporates a few basic exercises. There are tons of apps that can guide you through it; some are free. If you feel stronger or have more time, you can do 2 or 3 rounds. So, 3 times a week for 7 minutes equals 21 minutes. The best part is this can be done from the comfort of your bedroom, wearing your underwear. As for the other 30 minutes, go for a brisk 15-minute walk twice a week. That's it, there is your one hour a week. Utilize this time further by listening to an audio book or a podcast while you are walking or running.

The impact of exercise on the well-being of the body and mind is endless and documented. It is so central for your resilience that it cannot be skipped. It is a cornerstone.

Food

The other aspect of physical health, which ties directly into mental health, is the food that you eat. We sometimes underestimate how food impacts our energy levels. Have you ever noticed how you start feeling low around 3:00 p.m. and seek a sugary delight with some caffeine to pick you up? It is your body crashing after the carbs you had for lunch.

It seems that everybody has something to preach about what to eat these days. At some point or another, carbs, proteins, dairy, and fruits have either been the hero or the villain in our quest for good health, which is confusing and frustrating. I've come to realize that we should eat everything that this great planet of ours offers us, but in moderation. What I mean by that is, we should be smart about it. Carbs are good when you combine them with some vegetables. Protein is also necessary, but not when piled with pasta.

The basic principles are these:

1. Never ever eat your fill.
   Always leave some room in your stomach.

2. It's not about what you take out, but what you put in your diet that matters.
   So instead of dragging your feet or stressing over what you should cut out of your diet, think about what you need to have more of and start with that. So, start with a salad before a big meal; it will

help reduce the quantity of the unhealthier items you are about to consume.

3. Eat food that gives you energy.
   For some, it could be a triple burger with a salad; for others, it could be a cheese sandwich. All bodies are not created equal. Use the journal and figure out what fills you with energy and eat more of it.

4. Be careful which food you combine:
5. If you want to increase your energy, consider:
   • Protein with vegetables (one or two kinds of vegetables max) the lesser the variety the better.
   • Carbs with vegetables (one or two kinds of vegetables max)
6. If you desire lethargy and a good nap after a meal (i.e., please avoid!)
7. Proteins and carbs, e.g. steak and potato
8. Fruits after a meal
9. Soft drinks. Enough said on that topic.
10. Sugar that comes in the form of desserts, candy bars, soft drinks, and more. Watch out for it; the less you consume, the better.
11. Mixing proteins, e.g. you are at a barbeque and have fish, chicken, and beef, even if it's just a bit of each. Your body processes each food differently and will take longer to process the different kinds.

12. Limit your caffeine intake (coffee and sodas)
    Coffee really isn't good for you. You shouldn't exceed a cup a day. Ideally, 2 to 3 cups of coffee a week. I can almost feel the rage in some of you at this statement: "How do you expect me to wake up?" Well, you have to ask yourself what coffee does for you and why you need it. Is it a habit? Or is your body accustomed to it? Research has proven that for serial coffee drinkers it affects them contrarily from what they expect. It slows them down and

has minor effects on them. That's why they tend to drink more, presuming that the increased quantity gives the desired effect of alertness.

13. Drink lots of water. Your daily intake should ideally be 30 ml per kilo or half an ounce per pound of your weight. For example, if your weight is 100 kg (220 lbs.), your daily water intake should be 3 liters (110 fl. oz.).

14. Educate yourself about what food does to your body and, more importantly, how they are produced. There is a lot of information in this field.

15. Finally, try to eat organic. It's slightly pricier but incrementally better for your health.

Rituals for the Health of the SPIRIT

Spiritual health is a sensitive topic to most; often we tie it with religious beliefs, but it has nothing to do with religion. What I mean by spiritual health is our interaction with the world around us. In one simple word, it's about *Giving!*

We must recognize that we humans are all related to one another. Unfortunately, not always in good relations, but relations nevertheless. Our spirit grows as we feed it, and we feed it with giving. Giving is practiced in a multitude of situations, like random acts of kindness, pleasant words for the people we meet, or those who serve us in restaurants or on flights. A genuine smile for someone who feels left out is another form of giving.

While charitable work and donations are a classic form of giving, it is important not to assume they are the only legitimate method of giving. You can give daily, with modest acts that require practically no effort.

Make it a habit to give at least once a day, judge how that makes you feel, and maybe with time, you will give more.

The Corporate Mindset

The corporate mindset is an extension of its leadership's mindset. The line from "Remember the Titans" rings true: "Attitude Reflects Leadership." In other words:

- Your company will take decisions the way you take decisions. So, if you analyze information, they will analyze; if you take decisions on a whim, the company will do the same. Watch out for how you are telling your company to behave and apply a growth mindset that accepts and includes varied methods of taking decisions.
- If you set goals, your company will set goals. If you review them every 2 months, the company will do the same.
- If you consume healthy information and share it with your team, they will also mimic that.

As a leader, the company becomes an extension of you! Be a stellar role model.

Final Words

At the end of this chapter, I have included a form that would help you carry out an annual or semi-annual assessment of how you have lived over the past year. Checking one's self is always a beneficial practice that ensures you stay on track and manage yourself. In addition, there is a form to help you assess your business.

Additional Sources of Information

- Book: *Think and Grow Rich* by Napoleon Hill
- Book: *Never Be Sick Again* by Raymond Francis
- Book: *Mindset* by Carol Dweck
- Book: *Tools for Titans* Tim Ferriss

- TED talk: Amy Cuddy, Your Body Language May Shape Who You Are
- Forms are available online at: www.breakingceilings.com/forms

Health-check Assessment

Criteria	A	B	C
How often do you exercise?	At least 3 times a week	Once or twice a month	Whenever I have time
Do you eat vegetables regularly?	Practically with every meal	Daily salad	I'm not giving up my burger!
Do you consume alcohol?	Never	2–3 times a week	More than 3 times a week
Do you smoke?	Never	Socially	Regularly
What time do you wake up every day?	Before 6:00 a.m.	Before 7:00 a.m.	8:00 a.m. or after
Do you meditate?	Yes, every day	Yes, occasionally	No
Do you have annual goals?	Yes	They are in my head.	No
Do you attend any training courses, conferences, or functions that you learn from or are you exposed to new ideas? How many?	At least 3 annually	Once or twice a year	I know everything I need.
Do you have scheduled thinking time? (Time where you sit without any sort of interruption and think about a certain topic)	Regularly, at least twice a week	Occasionally, whenever I have a serious problem to resolve	Who has time to think?
Do you regularly read books on various topics? If yes, how many?	More than 20 per year	2–19 per year	I rarely finish a book a year.
Do you regularly read, listen, or watch industry-related materials, trade journals, podcasts, videos?	It's part of my daily routine.	A few times a month	Rarely

Criteria	A	B	C
Do you assess your achievements every year?	Like clockwork	Sometimes	Not really
Do you take decisions based on analysis and reflection?	Always with few exceptions	50/50	I have a hard time making up my mind and just go with my gut.
Do you stick to a personal budget?	I have an app to track all my expenses.	For the big-ticket items only	It kind of works out on its own.
Do you have a master-mind group (group of trusted advisors)?	We meet regularly.	I have 1 or 2 advisors whom I call occasionally.	Google is my best advisor.
Do you have a personal mantra or goal statement?	Yes, and I read it aloud every day.	Yes, and I occasionally check it.	No
Are you in control of your days?	All the time	50/50	My days are chaotic.
Do you feel energized by what you do?	I'm on fire.	I have my good and bad days.	I am always exhausted.
Do you support charities with your time?	Regularly	Every once in a while	Not really
Do you donate to charity?	Regularly	Every once in a while	Not really, only for tax breaks
Do you have clear values by which you live your life?	I recite them every day	I know them but have never written them down.	I do what I need to survive.
Are you kind to strangers?	Always	Depends what they want	Don't have time for them
Do you go to networking events?	Regularly, at least once a week	Occasionally, 2–3 times per month	I don't have time for them.
Do you spend quality time with your family and friends?	Regularly, I schedule it in my calendar.	I do my best but it's hard.	I see my family on the weekends.
Do you generally feel energized and aligned?	Most of the time	Some of the time	Rarely

Number of A answers	_____	X	3	_____
Number of B answers	_____	X	2	_____
Number of C answers	_____	X	1	
		Your Total Score		

Annual Health Check Assessment

Criteria	Yes	Partial	No
• Did I live in harmony with my values?			
• Were most of my decisions based on feelings/gut or proper analysis?			
• Did I consistently pursue my goals and manage to control self-doubt and fear?			
• Was I open to new ideas, experiences throughout the year, or did I stick to my old ways? If yes, what were those new ideas?			
• Did I meet my annual objectives?			
• Was I in control of my mornings?			
• Was I in control of my days?			
• Did I prepare a clear set of goals for the year and a map of how I would achieve them?			
• Did I follow the map?			
• Did my job/business energize and inspire me?			
• Did I enhance my knowledge? How?			
• How many seminars, conferences, and trainings did I attend?			
• Did I exercise at least thrice a week?			
• Did my mind control what I ate?			
• Did I have regular 20–30 minute "Thinking Time" sessions (at least twice a week)?			
• Did I exert physical effort in helping those in need? How much time?			
• Did I spend some of my money helping those in need? How much money?			

Criteria	Yes	Partial	No
• Did I feel comfortable for most of the year?			
• Do the people whom I regularly see energize and challenge me or do they cut me down and drain me?			
• How many books did I read? List the subjects.			
• Did I record my personal expenses and stick to a budget?			
• Did I improve/enrich the lives of others through my job/business?			
• Did I improve/enrich the lives of others in my community?			
• How many new people did I meet this year?			
• Did I communicate with them, either directly, or as part of a group, at least twice this year?			
• Did I consistently respect others?			
• Did I spend quality time with my children, spouse, significant other, family? Explain.			
• Did I have a mastermind group? And did I engage them at least once a week?			

Number of Yes answers _____ x 3 _____

Number of Partial answers _____ x 2 _____

Number of No answers _____ x 1

Your Total Score [ ]

HORIZON OF EXIT—*FUTURE*

HORIZON OF EXIT

As a business owner, you must have received advice at some point about having an exit strategy and how important it is to have one. This conversation on exiting the business is a useful one to have, but there's more to it than that.

First, if it is only a discussion on exit strategy, then the answer is direct: you sell the business, give it to your children, or wind it down. I cannot think of any other way to exit a business.

Second, why would you want to get rid of a business that is doing well? If you have a business that is providing a steady stream of cash flow and is working smoothly, it begs the question: why would you exit it? There are the obvious reasons: health, retirement, etc., and very little otherwise.

Unfortunately, the discussion about exit is usually framed in an unfavorable context. While it is a topic that every business owner should be thinking about, it is not thought of in the right context. When it comes to setting a favorable frame in the context of exit, I believe Keith J. Cunningham stated it perfectly: "Run your business like you're keeping it forever and could sell it tomorrow if you wanted."

What that essentially means is that we should contemplate the ability to exit, but not necessarily make it an end goal. If you think of your business from that context, I believe it gives an altered perspective on how you run it.

Still not convinced? Well, answer this question; **Would you buy your own company? And for how much?**

Think about it! Would you be willing to pay that much for your business? You see, it is very easy for us to get emotionally attached and not see the big picture, but if an outsider comes in tomorrow and says, "You know what, I'm going to buy your business. Show me your books; tell me about your operations," would they actually buy your business? And how much would they offer?

What Keith said is quite powerful: *"The only way you can command the price that you have in your mind for your business is if it is generating free cash flow, maintains good reports, employs people who are well- trained, feeds a culture that supports its operations and much more."*

As we reach the conclusion of *Breaking Ceilings*, I wish to leave you with some thoughts on how to move on from here:

1. **Annual Calendar**
   Prepare an annual calendar in which you include all the key events of the year. Things like when you are going to conduct the risk assessments, when reports are due, when to check-in with key customers, board meetings, staff meetings, etc.

   It will keep you focused on what is important.

2. **Culture**
   Keep an eye on how the culture of your business is developing, any behaviors or incidents. Act swiftly to correct any occurrences that threaten it.

3. Health, Yours!

Stay healthy. Your family and business depend on you, and more importantly, you need to enjoy your journey. There is greatly more enjoyment when you have a healthy body, mind, and soul. It is contagious, and you will be doing a lot of people a favor by being that way.

4. Measure, Check, Adjust, Repeat

Measure the right indicators; check if you are still on the predetermined path and then adjust the levers and behaviors where needed. When you are all done with that, repeat it again.

5. Gut vs. Fact

Gut is important to have; it's that survival instinct, hunch, etc. But it should never ever take over facts. The most successful business people are driven by facts and analysis. They are ruthlessly disciplined in following their principles. Don't forego your principles solely because your gut tells you so.

6. Strategy

It is just that, a strategy. It needs to be checked and assessed repeatedly throughout a year, not annually. Strategy is your predetermined path; always make sure it is the right one.

7. Training

You can't ask somebody who's walking around with a broken leg to climb Mt. Everest. That person needs to be in peak shape for that to happen.

8. My Business, My Baby

Your business is not your baby. It is a source of economic benefit. No matter how you love it, it does not love you back. Your baby does. Remember that. You are not your business!

9. **Earnings vs. Cash Flow**

It is not how much money you make; it is how much of your money you keep!

10. **Failures**

Celebrate them! Learn from them! Keep them in a log so everyone will learn.

11. **Customers**

Stay close to your customers. Know them more than they know themselves. Your product will sell itself.

12. **Play the long term**

Keep your eye on the long-term benefits, and don't give them up for short-term gains.

Go forth and prosper. Good luck.

AFTERWORD

Dear Reader,

Words cannot express my gratitude for the time you have invested in reading this book. My only hope is that somewhere in these pages you have found the information that will help you in breaking your current ceiling and every other limitation you may come across.

The book's inception came from years of frustration wrought by observing the costly mistakes made by business owners, mistakes that could have been avoided. I have aimed to distil as much knowledge from my own experiences in these pages as possible.

I encourage you to go back through these chapters and run the exercises in order to gain more clarity on the different ways of looking at a business.

Aside from the technical aspects I've provided, there is a final quote that I believe will be a guiding light in your moments of turbulence by Ray Dalio (CEO of Bridgewater):

> *All successful people operate by principles that help them be successful. Without principles you would be forced to react to circumstances that come at you without considering what you value the most and how to*

make choices to get you what you want. This will prevent you from making the most of your life. While operating without principles is bad for individuals, it is even worse for groups of individuals, such as companies. Because it leads to people randomly bumping into each other without understanding their own values and how to behave in order to be consistent with those values.

In our principles lie the secrets to achieving all goals we set our eyes upon. Spend the time to set your principles, be clear about them, and don't be shy in communicating them to the people around you. Though we may live in a world where principles are being eroded, I genuinely believe in the power of business, specifically small and medium businesses, to rebuild the good principles we so desperately need in our world's present climate.

Thank you, and may you and your business thrive and persevere!

—THE END—